W9-BTJ-551

THE ALDINE EDITION

OF THE BRITISH

POETS

THE POEMS OF GEOFFREY CHAUCER

IN SIX VOLUMES

VOL II

THE
POETICAL WORKS OF
GEOFFREY CHAUCER

WITH MEMOIR BY SIR HARRIS NICOLAS

VOL II

LONDON
WILLIAM PICKERING
1845

CONTENTS.

VOL. II.

THE CANTERBURY TALES.

CONTENTS.

VOL. II.

The Canterbury Tales.

THE CANTERBURY TALES.

The Prologue.

WHANNE that April with his shoures sote
The droughte of March hath perced to the
And bathed every veine in swiche licour, [rote,
Of whiche vertue engendred is the flour;
Whan Zephirus eke with his sote brethe
Enspired hath in every holt and hethe
The tendre croppes, and the yonge sonne
Hath in the Ram his halfe cours yronne,
And smale foules maken melodie,
That slepen alle night with open eye,
So priketh hem nature in hir corages;
Than longen folk to gon on pilgrimages,
And palmeres for to seken strange strondes,
To serve halwes couthe in sondry londes;
And specially, from every shires ende
Of Englelond, to Canterbury they wende,
The holy blisful martyr for to seke,
That hem hath holpen, whan that they were seke.
  Befelle, that, in that seson on a day,
In Southwerk at the Tabard as I lay,
Redy to wenden on my pilgrimage
To Canterbury with devoute corage,
At night was come into that hostelrie
Wel nine and twenty in a compagnie

1   B

Of sondry folk, by aventure yfalle
In felawship, and pilgrimes were they alle,
That toward Canterbury wolden ride.
The chambres and the stables weren wide,
And wel we weren esed atte beste.

   And shortly, whan the sonne was gon to reste,
So hadde I spoken with hem everich on,
That I was of hir felawship anon,
And made forword erly for to rise,
To take oure way ther as I you devise.

   But natheles, while I have time and space,
Or that I forther in this tale pace,
Me thinketh it accordant to reson,
To tellen you alle the condition
Of eche of hem, so as it semed me,
And whiche they weren, and of what degre ;
And eke in what araie that they were inne :
And at a knight than wol I firste beginne.

   A KNIGHT ther was, and that a worthy man,
That fro the time that he firste began
To riden out, he loved chevalrie,
Trouthe and honour, fredom and curtesie.
Ful worthy was he in his lordes werre,
And therto hadde he ridden, no man ferre,
As wel in Cristendom as in Hethenesse,
And ever honoured for his worthinesse.

   At Alisandre he was whan it was wonne.
Ful often time he hadde the bord begonne,
Aboven alle nations, in Pruce.
In Lettowe hadde he reysed and in Ruce,
No cristen man so ofte of his degre.
In Gernade at the siege eke hadde he be
Of Algesir, and ridden in Belmarie.
At Leyes was he, and at Satalie,

Whan they were wonne; and in the Grete see
At many a noble armee hadde he be.
At mortal batailles hadde he ben fiftene,
And foughten for our faith at Tramissene
In listes thries, and ay slain his fo.

This ilke worthy knight hadde ben also
Somtime with the lord of Palatie,
Agen another hethen in Turkie:
And evermore he hadde a sovereine pris.
And though that he was worthy he was wise,
And of his port as meke as is a mayde.
He never yet no vilanie ne sayde
In alle his lif, unto no manere wight.
He was a veray parfit gentil knight.

But for to tellen you of his araie,
His hors was good, but he ne was not gaie.
Of fustian he wered a gipon,
Alle besmotred with his habergeon,
For he was late ycome fro his viage,
And wente for to don his pilgrimage.

With him ther was his sone a yonge SQUIER,
A lover, and a lusty bacheler,
With lockes crull as they were laide in presse.
Of twenty yere of age he was I gesse.
Of his stature he was of even lengthe,
And wonderly deliver, and grete of strengthe.
And he hadde be somtime in chevachie,
In Flaundres, in Artois, and in Picardie,
And borne him wel, as of so litel space,
In hope to stonden in his ladies grace.

Embrouded was he, as it were a mede
Alle ful of fresshe floures, white and rede.
Singing he was, or floyting alle the day,
He was as fresshe, as is the moneth of May.

Short was his goune, with sleves long and wide.
Wel coude he sitte on hors, and fayre ride.
He coude songes make, and wel endite,
Juste and eke dance, and wel pourtraie and write.
So hote he loved, that by nightertale
He slep no more than doth the nightingale.

    Curteis he was, lowly, and servisable,
And carf before his fader at the table.

    A YEMAN hadde he, and servantes no mo
At that time, for him luste to ride so;
And he was cladde in cote and hode of grene.
A shefe of peacock arwes bright and kene
Under his belt he bare ful thriftily.
Wel coude he dresse his takel yemanly:
His arwes drouped not with fetheres lowe.
And in his hond he bare a mighty bowe.

    A not-hed hadde he, with a broune visage.
Of wood-craft coude he wel alle the usage.
Upon his arme he bare a gaie bracer,
And by his side a swerd and a bokeler,
And on that other side a gaie daggere,
Harneised wel, and sharpe as point of spere:
A Cristofre on his brest of silver shene.
An horne he bare, the baudrik was of grene.
A forster was he sothely as I gesse.

    Ther was also a Nonne, a PRIORESSE,
That of hire smiling was ful simple and coy;
Hire gretest othe n'as but by Seint Eloy;
And she was cleped madame Eglentine.
Ful wel she sange the service devine,
Entuned in hire nose ful swetely;
And Frenche she spake ful fayre and fetisly,
After the scole of Stratford-atte-bowe,
For Frenche of Paris was to hire unknowe.

At mete was she wel ytaughte withalle ;
She lette no morsel from hire lippes falle,
Ne wette hire fingres in hire sauce depe.
Wel coude she carie a morsel, and wel kepe,
Thatte no drope ne fell upon hire brest.
In curtesie was sette ful moche hire lest.
Hire over lippe wiped she so clene,
That in hire cuppe was no ferthing sene
Of grese, whan she dronken hadde hire draught.
Ful semely after hire mete she raught.
And sikerly she was of grete disport,
And ful plesant, and amiable of port,
And peined hire to contrefeten chere
Of court, and ben estatelich of manere,
And to ben holden digne of reverence.

But for to speken of hire conscience,
She was so charitable and so pitous,
She wolde wepe if that she saw a mous
Caughte in a trappe, if it were ded or bledde.
Of smale houndes hadde she, that she fedde
With rosted flesh, and milk, and wastel brede.
But sore wept she if on of hem were dede,
Or if men smote it with a yerde smert :
And all was conscience and tendre herte.

Ful semely hire wimple ypinched was ;
Hire nose tretis ; hire eyen grey as glas ;
Hire mouth ful smale, and therto soft and red ;
But sikerly she hadde a fayre forehed.
It was almost a spanne brode I trowe ;
For hardily she was not undergrowe.

Ful fetise was hire cloke, as I was ware.
Of smale corall aboute hire arm she bare
A pair of bedes, gauded all with grene ;
And theron heng a broche of gold ful shene,

On whiche was first ywriten a crouned A,
And after, *Amor vincit omnia.*

   Another NONNE also with hire hadde she,
That was hire chapelleine, and PREESTES thre.

   A MONK ther was, a fayre for the maistrie,
An out-rider, that loved venerie;
A manly man, to ben an abbot able.
Ful many a deinte hors hadde he in stable:
And whan he rode, men mighte his bridel here
Gingeling in a whistling wind as clere,
And eke as loude, as doth the chapell belle,
Ther as this lord was keper of the celle.

   The reule of seint Maure and of seint Beneit,
Because that it was olde and somdele streit,
This ilke monk lette olde thinges pace,
And held after the newe world the trace.
He yave not of the text a pulled hen,
That saith, that hunters ben not holy men;
Ne that a monk, whan he is rekkeles,
Is like to a fish that is waterles;
This is to say, a monk out of his cloistre.
This ilke text held he not worth an oistre.
And I say his opinion was good.
What shulde he studie, and make himselven wood,
Upon a book in cloistre alway to pore,
Or swinken with his hondes, and laboure,
As Austin bit? how shal the world be served?
Let Austin have his swink to him reserved.
Therfore he was a prickasoure a right:
Greihoundes he hadde as swift as foul of flight:
Of pricking and of hunting for the hare
Was all his lust, for no cost wolde he spare.

   I saw his sleves purfiled at the hond
With gris, and that the finest of the lond.

And for to fasten his hood under his chinne,
He hadde of gold ywrought a curious pinne:
A love-knotte in the greter end ther was.
His hed was balled, and shone as any glas,
And eke his face, as it hadde ben anoint.
He was a lord ful fat and in good point.
His eyen stepe, and rolling in his hed,
That stemed as a forneis of a led.
His botes souple, his hors in gret estat,
Now certainly he was a fayre prelat.
He was not pale as a forpined gost.
A fat swan loved he best of any rost.
His palfrey was as broune as is a bery.

A FRERE ther was, a wanton and a mery,
A Limitour, a ful solempne man.
In all the ordres foure is non that can
So moche of daliance and fayre langage.
He hadde ymade ful many a mariage
Of yonge wimmen, at his owen cost.
Until his ordre he was a noble post.
Ful wel beloved, and familier was he
With frankeleins over all in his contree,
And eke with worthy wimmen of the toun:
For he had power of confession,
As saide himselfe, more than a curat,
For of his ordre he was licenciat.
Ful swetely herde he confession,
And plesant was his absolution.
He was an esy man to give penance,
Ther as he wiste to han a good pitance:
For unto a poure ordre for to give
Is signe that a man is wel yshrive.
For if he gave, he dorste make avant,
He wiste that a man was repentant.

For many a man so hard is of his herte,
He may not wepe although him sore smerte.
Therfore in stede of weping and praieres,
Men mote give silver to the poure freres.

His tippet was ay farsed ful of knives,
And pinnes, for to given fayre wives.
And certainly he hadde a mery note.
Wel coude he singe and plaien on a rote.
Of yeddinges he bare utterly the pris.
His nekke was white as the flour de lis.
Therto he strong was as a champioun,
And knew wel the tavernes in every toun,
And every hosteler and gay tapstere,
Better than a lazar or a beggere,
For unto swiche a worthy man as he
Accordeth nought, as by his faculte,
To haven with sike lazars acquaintance.
It is not honest, it may not avance,
As for to delen with no swiche pouraille,
But all with riche, and sellers of vitaille.

And over all, ther as profit shuld arise,
Curteis he was, and lowly of servise.
Ther n'as no man nowher so vertuous.
He was the beste begger in all his hous:
And gave a certaine ferme for the grant,
Non of his bretheren came in his haunt.
For though a widewe hadde but a shoo,
(So plesant was his *In principio*)
Yet wold he have a ferthing or he went.
His pourchas was wel better than his rent.
And rage he coude as it hadde ben a whelp,
In lovedayes, ther coude he mochel help.
For ther was he nat like a cloisterere,
With thredbare cope, as is a poure scolere,

But he was like a maister or a pope.
Of double worsted was his semicope,
That round was as a belle out of the presse.
Somwhat he lisped for his wantonnesse,
To make his English swete upon his tonge ;
And in his harping, whan that he hadde songe,
His eyen twinkeled in his hed aright,
As don the sterres in a frosty night.
This worthy limitour was cleped Huberd.

A MARCHANT was ther with a forked berd,
In mottelee, and highe on hors he sat,
And on his hed a Flaundrish bever hat.
His botes clapsed fayre and fetisly.
His resons spake he ful solempnely,
Souning alway the encrese of his winning.
He wold the see were kept for any thing
Betwixen Middelburgh and Orewell.
Wel coud he in eschanges sheldes selle.
This worthy man ful wel his wit besette ;
Ther wiste no wight that he was in dette,
So stedefastly didde he his governance,
With his bargeines, and with his chevisance.
Forsothe he was a worthy man withalle,
But soth to sayn, I n'ot how men him calle.

A CLERK ther was of Oxenforde also,
That unto logike hadde long ygo.
As lene was his hors as is a rake,
And he was not right fat, I undertake ;
But loked holwe, and therto soberly.
Ful thredbare was his overest courtepy,
For he hadde geten him yet no benefice,
Ne was nought worldly to have an office.
For him was lever han at his beddes hed
A twenty bokes, clothed in black or red,

Of Aristotle, and his philosophie,
Than robes riche, or fidel, or sautrie.
But all be that he was a philosophre,
Yet hadde he but litel gold in cofre,
But all that he might of his frendes hente,
On bokes and on lerning he it spente,
And besily gan for the soules praie
Of hem, that yave him wherwith to scolaie.
Of studie toke he moste cure and hede.
Not a word spake he more than was nede;
And that was said in forme and reverence,
And short and quike, and ful of high sentence.
Souning in moral vertue was his speche,
And gladly wolde he lerne, and gladly teche.

A SERGEANT OF THE LAWE ware and wise,
That often hadde yben at the paruis,
Ther was also, ful riche of excellence.
Discrete he was, and of gret reverence:
He semed swiche, his wordes were so wise,
Justice he was ful often in assise,
By patent, and by pleine commissioun;
For his science, and for his high renoun,
Of fees and robes had he many on.
So grete a pourchasour was nowher non.
All was fee simple to him in effect,
His pourchasing might not ben in suspect.
Nowher so besy a man as he ther n'as,
And yet he semed besier than he was.
In termes hadde he cas and domes alle,
That fro the time of king Will. weren falle.
Therto he coude endite, and make a thing,
Ther coude no wight pinche at his writing.
And every statute coude he plaine by rote.
He rode but homely in a medlee cote,

Girt with a seint of silk, with barres smale ;
Of his array tell I no lenger tale.

A FRANKELEIN was in this compagnie ;
White was his berd, as is the dayesie.
Of his complexion he was sanguin.
Wel loved he by the morwe a sop in win.
To liven in delit was ever his wone,
For he was Epicures owen sone,
That held opinion, that plein delit
Was veraily felicite parfite.
An housholder, and that a grete was he ;
Seint Julian he was in his contree.
His brede, his ale, was alway after on ;
A better envyned man was no wher non.
Withouten bake mete never was his hous,
Of fish and flesh, and that so plenteous,
It snewed in his hous of mete and drinke,
Of alle deintees that men coud of thinke,
After the sondry sesons of the yere,
So changed he his mete and his soupere.
Ful many a fat partrich hadde he in mewe,
And many a breme, and many a luce in stewe.
Wo was his coke, but if his sauce were
Poinant and sharpe, and redy all his gere.
His table dormant in his halle alway
Stode redy covered alle the longe day.

At sessions ther was he lord and sire.
Ful often time he was knight of the shire.
An anelace and a gipciere all of silk,
Heng at his girdel, white as morwe milk.
A shereve hadde he ben, and a countour.
Was no wher swiche a worthy vavasour.

An HABERDASHER, and a CARPENTER,
A WEBBE, a DEYER, and a TAPISER,

Were alle yclothed in o livere,
Of a solempne and grete fraternite.
Ful freshe and newe hir gere ypiked was.
Hir knives were ychaped not with bras,
But all with silver wrought ful clene and wel,
Hir girdeles and hir pouches every del.
Wel semed eche of hem a fayre burgeis,
To sitten in a gild halle, on the deis.
Everich, for the wisdom that he can,
Was shapelich for to ben an alderman.
For catel hadden they ynough and rent,
And eke hir wives wolde it wel assent:
And elles certainly they were to blame.
It is ful fayre to ben ycleped madame,
And for to gon to vigiles all before,
And have a mantel reallich ybore.

  A Coke they hadden with hem for the nones,
To boile the chikenes and the marie bones,
And poudre marchant, tart and galingale.
Wel coude he knowe a draught of London ale.
He coude roste, and sethe, and broile, and frie,
Maken mortrewes, and wel bake a pie.
But gret harm was it, as it thoughte me,
That on his shinne a mormal hadde he.
For blanc manger that made he with the best.

  A Shipman was ther, woned fer by West:
For ought I wote, he was of Dertemouth.
He rode upon a rouncie, as he couthe,
All in a goune of falding to the knee.
A dagger hanging by a las hadde hee
About his nekke under his arm adoun.
The hote sommer hadde made his hewe al broun.
And certainly he was a good felaw.
Ful many a draught of win he hadde draw

From Burdeux ward, while that the chapman
Of nice conscience toke he no kepe.   [slepe.
If that he faught, and hadde the higher hand,
By water he sent hem home to every land.
But of his craft to reken wel his tides,
His stremes and his strandes him besides,
His herberwe, his mone, and his lodemanage,
Ther was non swiche, from Hull unto Cartage.
Hardy he was, and wise, I undertake:
With many a tempest hadde his berd be shake.
He knew wel alle the havens, as they were,
Fro Gotland, to the Cape de Finistere,
And every creke in Bretagne and in Spaine:
His barge ycleped was the Magdelaine.

   With us ther was a DOCTOUR OF PHISIKE,
In all this world ne was ther non him like
To speke of phisike, and of surgerie:
For he was grounded in astronomie.
He kept his patient a ful gret del
In houres by his magike naturel.
Wel coude he fortunen the ascendent
Of his images for his patient.
   He knew the cause of every maladie,
Were it of cold, or hote, or moist, or drie,
And wher engendred, and of what humour,
He was a veray parfite practisour.
The cause yknowe, and of his harm the rote,
Anon he gave to the sike man his bote.
Ful redy hadde he his apothecaries
To send him dragges, and his lettuaries,
For eche of hem made other for to winne:
Hir frendship n'as not newe to beginne.
Wel knew he the old Esculapius,
And Dioscorides, and eke Rufus;

Old Hippocras, Hali, and Gallien;
Serapion, Rasis, and Avicen;
Averrois, Damascene, and Constantin;
Bernard, and Gatisden, and Gilbertin.
Of his diete mesurable was he,
For it was of no superfluitee,
But of gret nourishing, and digestible.
His studie was but litel on the Bible.
In sanguin and in perse he clad was alle
Lined with taffata, and with sendalle.
And yet he was but esy of dispence:
He kepte that he wan in the pestilence.
For gold in phisike is a cordial;
Therfore he loved gold in special.

    A good Wif was ther of beside Bathe,
But she was som del defe, and that was scathe.
Of cloth making she hadde swiche an haunt,
She passed hem of Ipres, and of Gaunt.
In all the parish wif ne was ther non,
That to the offring before hire shulde gon,
And if ther did, certain so wroth was she,
That she was out of alle charitee.
Hire coverchiefs weren ful fine of ground;
I dorste swere, they weyeden a pound;
That on the Sonday were upon hire hede.
Hire hosen weren of fine scarlet rede,
Ful streite yteyed, and shoon ful moist and newe.
Bold was hire face, and fayre and rede of hew.
She was a worthy woman all hire live,
Housbondes at the chirche dore had she had five,
Withouten other compagnie in youthe.
But therof nedeth not to speke as nouthe.
And thries hadde she ben at Jerusaleme.
She hadde passed many a strange streme.

At Rome she hadde ben, and at Boloine,
In Galice at Seint James, and at Coloine.
She coude moche of wandring by the way.
Gat-tothed was she, sothly for to say.
Upon an ambler esily she sat,
Ywimpled wel, and on hire hede an hat,
As brode as is a bokeler, or a targe.
A fote-mantel about hire hippes large,
And on hire fete a pair of sporres sharpe.
In felawship wel coude she laughe and carpe
Of remedies of love she knew parchance,
For of that arte she coude the olde dance.

  A good man ther was of religioun,
That was a poure PERSONE of a toun:
But riche he was of holy thought and werk.
He was also a lerned man, a clerk,
That Cristes gospel trewely wolde preche.
His parishens devoutly wolde he teche.
Benigne he was, and wonder diligent,
And in adversite ful patient:
And swiche he was ypreved often sithes.
Ful loth were him to cursen for his tithes,
But rather wolde he yeven out of doute,
Unto his poure parishens aboute,
Of his offring, and eke of his substance.
He coude in litel thing have suffisance.
Wide was his parish, and houses fer asonder,
But he ne left nought for no rain ne thonder,
In sikenesse and in mischief to visite
The ferrest in his parish, moche and lite,
Upon his fete, and in his hand a staf.
This noble ensample to his shepe he yaf,
That first he wrought, and afterward he taught.
Out of the gospel he the wordes caught,

And this figure he added yet therto,
That if gold ruste, what shuld iren do?
For if a preest be foule, on whom we trust,
No wonder is a lewed man to rust:
And shame it is, if that a preest take kepe,
To see a shitten shepherd, and clene shepe:
Wel ought a preest ensample for to yeve,
By his clenenesse, how his shepe shulde live.

   He sette not his benefice to hire,
And lette his shepe acombred in the mire,
And ran unto London, unto Seint Poules,
To seken him a chanterie for soules,
Or with a brotherhede to be withold:
But dwelt at home, and kepte wel his fold,
So that the wolf ne made it not miscarie.
He was a shepherd, and no mercenarie.
And though he holy were, and vertuous,
He was to sinful men not dispitous,
Ne of his speche dangerous ne digne,
But in his teching discrete and benigne.
To drawen folk to heven, with fairenesse,
By good ensample, was his besinesse:
But it were any persone obstinat,
What so he were of highe, or low estat,
Him wolde he snibben sharply for the nones.
A better preest I trowe that nowher non is.
He waited after no pompe ne reverence,
Ne maked him no spiced conscience,
But Cristes lore, and his apostles twelve,
He taught, but first he folwed it himselve.

   With him ther was a PLOWMAN, was his brother,
That hadde ylaid of dong ful many a fother.
A trewe swinker, and a good was he,
Living in pees, and parfite charitee.

God loved he beste with alle his herte
At alle times, were it gain or smerte,
And than his neighebour right as himselve.
He wolde thresh, and therto dike, and delve,
For Cristes sake, for every poure wight,
Withouten hire, if it lay in his might.

His tithes paied he ful fayre and wel
Both of his propre swinke, and his catel.
In a tabard he rode upon a mere.

Ther was also a reve, and a millere,
A sompnour, and a pardoner also,
A manciple, and myself, ther n'ere no mo.

The MILLER was a stout carl for the nones,
Ful bigge he was of braun, and eke of bones;
That proved wel, for over all ther he came,
At wrastling he wold bere away the ram.
He was short shuldered brode, a thikke gnarre,
Ther n'as no dore, that he n'olde heve of barre,
Or breke it at a renning with his hede.
His berd as any sowe or fox was rede,
And therto brode, as though it were a spade.
Upon the cop right of his nose he hade
A wert, and theron stode a tufte of heres,
Rede as the bristles of a sowes eres.
His nose-thirles blacke were and wide.
A swerd and bokeler bare he by his side.
His mouth as wide was as a forneis.
He was a jangler, and a goliardeis,
And that was most of sinne, and harlotries.
Wel coude he stelen corne, and tollen thries.
And yet he had a thomb of gold parde.
A white cote and a blew hode wered he.
A baggepipe wel coude he blowe and soune,
And therwithall he brought us out of toune.

A gentil MANCIPLE was ther of a temple,
Of which achatours mighten take ensemple
For to ben wise in bying of vitaille.
For whether that he paide, or toke by taille,
Algate he waited so in his achate,
That he was ay before in good estate.
Now is not that of God a ful fayre grace,
That swiche a lewed mannes wit shal pace
The wisdom of an hepe of lered men?

Of maisters had he mo than thries ten,
That were of lawe expert and curious:
Of which ther was a dosein in that hous,
Worthy to ben stewardes of rent and lond
Of any lord that is in Englelond,
To maken him live by his propre good,
In honour detteles, but if he were wood,
Or live as scarsly, as him list desire;
And able for to helpen all a shire
In any cas that mighte fallen or happe;
And yet this manciple sette hir aller cappe.

The REVE was a slendre colerike man,
His berd was shave as neighe as ever he can.
His here was by his eres round yshorne.
His top was docked like a preest beforne.
Ful longe were his legges, and ful lene,
Ylike a staff, ther was no calf ysene.
Wel coude he kepe a garner and a binne:
Ther was non auditour coude on him winne.
Wel wiste he by the drought, and by the rain,
The yelding of his seed, and of his grain.
His lordes shepe, his nete, and his deirie,
His swine, his hors, his store, and his pultrie,
Were holly in this reves governing,
And by his covenant yave he rekening,

Sin that his lord was twenty yere of age ;
Ther coude no man bring him in arerage.
Ther n'as baillif, ne herde, ne other hine,
That he ne knew his sleight and his covine :
They were adradde of him, as of the deth.
His wonning was ful fayre upon an heth,
With grene trees yshadewed was his place.
He coude better than his lord pourchace.
Ful riche he was ystored privily.
His lord wel coude he plesen subtilly,
To yeve and lene him of his owen good,
And have a thank, and yet a cote and hood.
In youthe he lerned hadde a good mistere.
He was a wel good wright, a carpentere.
This reve sate upon a right good stot,
That was all pomelee grey, and highte Scot.
A long surcote of perse upon he hade,
And by his side he bare a rusty blade.
Of Norfolk was this reve, of which I tell,
Beside a toun, men clepen Baldeswell.
Tucked he was, as is a frere, aboute,
And ever he rode the hinderest of the route.

A Sompnour was ther with us in that place,
That hadde a fire-red cherubinnes face,
For sausefleme he was, with eyen narwe.
As hote he was, and likerous as a sparwe,
With scalled browes blake, and pilled berd :
Of his visage children were sore aferd.
Ther n'as quiksilver, litarge, ne brimston,
Boras, ceruse, ne oile of tartre non,
Ne oinement that wolde clense or bite,
That him might helpen of his whelkes white,
Ne of the knobbes sitting on his chekes.
Wel loved he garlike, onions, and lekes,

And for to drinke strong win as rede as blood.
Than wolde he speke, and crie as he were wood.
And whan that he wel dronken had the win,
Than wold he speken no word but Latin.
A fewe termes coude he, two or three,
That he had lerned out of som decree;
No wonder is, he herd it all the day.
And eke ye knowen wel, how that a jay
Can clepen watte, as wel as can the pope.
But who so wolde in other thing him grope,
Than hadde he spent all his philosophie,
Ay, *Questio quid juris,* wolde he crie.

He was a gentil harlot and a kind;
A better felaw shulde a man not find.
He wolde suffre for a quart of wine,
A good felaw to have his concubine
A twelve month, and excuse him at the full.
Ful prively a finch eke coude he pull.
And if he found owhere a good felawe,
He wolde techen him to have non awe
In swiche a cas of the archedekenes curse;
But if a mannes soule were in his purse;
For in his purse he shulde ypunished be.
Purse is the archedekens helle, said he.
But wel I wote, he lied right in dede:
Of cursing ought eche gilty man him drede.
For curse wol sle right as assoiling saveth,
And also ware him of a *significavit.*

In danger hadde he at his owen gise
The yonge girles of the diocise,
And knew hir conseil, and was of hir rede.
A gerlond hadde he sette upon his hede,
As gret as it were for an alestake:
A bokeler hadde he made him of a cake.

With him ther rode a gentil PARDONERE
Of Rouncevall, his frend and his compere,
That streit was comen from the court of Rome.
Ful loude he sang, Come hither, love, to me.
This sompnour bare to him a stiff burdoun,
Was never trompe of half so gret a soun.
This pardoner had here as yelwe as wax,
But smoth it heng, as doth a strike of flax :
By unces heng his lokkes that he hadde,
And therwith he his shulders overspradde.
Ful thinne it lay, by culpons on and on,
But hode, for jolite, ne wered he non,
For it was trussed up in his wallet.
Him thought he rode al of the newe get,
Dishevele, sauf his cappe, he rode all bare.
Swiche glaring eyen hadde he, as an hare.
A vernicle hadde he sewed upon his cappe.
His wallet lay beforne him in his lappe,
Bret-ful of pardon come from Rome al hote.
A vois he hadde, as smale as hath a gote.
No berd hadde he, ne never non shulde have,
As smothe it was as it were newe shave ;
I trowe he were a gelding or a mare.

But of his craft, fro Berwike unto Ware,
Ne was ther swiche an other pardonere.
For in his male he hadde a pilwebere,
Which, as he saide, was oure ladies veil :
He saide, he hadde a gobbet of the seyl
Thatte seint Peter had, whan that he went
Upon the see, till Jesu Crist him hent.
He had a crois of laton ful of stones,
And in a glas he hadde pigges bones.
But with these relikes, whanne that he fond
A poure persone dwelling up on lond,

Upon a day he gat him more moneie
Than that the persone gat in monethes tweie.
And thus with fained flattering and japes,
He made the persone, and the peple, his apes.

But trewely to tellen atte last,
He was in chirche a noble ecclesiast.
Wel coude he rede a lesson or a storie,
But alderbest he sang an offertorie:
For wel he wiste, whan that song was songe,
He muste preche, and wel afile his tonge,
To winne silver, as he right wel coude:
Therfore he sang the merier and loude.

Now have I told you shortly in a clause,
Th'estat, th'araie, the nombre, and eke the cause
Why that assembled was this compagnie
In Southwerk at this gentil hostelrie,
That highte the Tabard, faste by the Belle.
But now is time to you for to telle,
How that we baren us that ilke night,
Whan we were in that hostelrie alight.
And after wol I telle of our viage,
And all the remenant of our pilgrimage.

But firste I praie you of your curtesie,
That ye ne arette it not my vilanie,
Though that I plainly speke in this matere,
To tellen you hir wordes and hir chere;
Ne though I speke hir wordes proprely.
For this ye knowen al so wel as I,
Who so shall telle a tale after a man,
He moste reherse, as neighe as ever he can,
Everich word, if it be in his charge,
All speke he never so rudely and so large;
Or elles he moste tellen his tale untrewe,
Or feinen thinges, or finden wordes newe.

He may not spare, although he were his brother.
He moste as wel sayn o word, as an other.
Crist spake himself ful brode in holy writ,
And wel ye wote no vilanie is it.
Eke Plato sayeth, who so can him rede,
The wordes moste ben cosin to the dede.

Also I praie you to forgive it me,
All have I not sette folk in hir degree,
Here in this tale, as that they shulden stonde.
My wit is short, ye may wel understonde.

Gret chere made oure hoste us everich on,
And to the souper sette he us anon:
And served us with vitaille of the beste.
Strong was the win, and wel to drinke us leste.
A semely man our hoste was with alle
For to han ben a marshal in an halle.
A large man he was with eyen stepe,
A fairer burgeis is ther non in Chepe:
Bold of his speche, and wise and wel ytaught,
And of manhood him lacked righte naught.
Eke therto was he right a mery man,
And after souper plaien he began,
And spake of mirthe amonges other thinges,
Whan that we hadden made our rekeninges;
And saide thus; Now, lordinges, trewely
Ye ben to me welcome right hertily:
For by my trouthe, if that I shal not lie,
I saw nat this yere swiche a compagnie
At ones in this herberwe, as is now.
Fayn wolde I do you mirthe, and I wiste how.
And of a mirthe I am right now bethought,
To don you ese, and it shall coste you nought.
Ye gon to Canterbury; God you spede,
The blisful martyr quite you your mede;

And wel I wot, as ye gon by the way,
Ye shapen you to talken and to play :
For trewely comfort ne mirthe is non,
To riden by the way dombe as the ston :
And therfore wold I maken you disport,
As I said erst, and don you some comfort.
And if you liketh alle by on assent
Now for to stonden at my jugement :
And for to werchen as I shal you say
To-morwe, whan ye riden on the way,
Now by my faders soule that is ded,
But ye be mery, smiteth of my hed.
Hold up your hondes withouten more speche.

    Our conseil was not longe for to seche :
Us thought it was not worth to make it wise,
And granted him withouten more avise,
And bad him say his verdit, as him leste.

    Lordinges, (quod he) now herkeneth for the
But take it nat, I pray you, in disdain ; [beste;
This is the point, to speke it plat and plain,
That eche of you to shorten with youre way,
In this viage, shal tellen tales tway,
To Canterbury ward, I mene it so,
And homeward he shall tellen other two,
Of aventures that whilom han befalle.
And which of you that bereth him best of alle,
That is to sayn, that telleth in this cas
Tales of best sentence and most solas,
Shal have a souper at youre aller cost
Here in this place sitting by this post,
Whan that ye comen agen from Canterbury.
And for to maken you the more mery,
I wol myselven gladly with you ride,
Right at min owen cost, and be your gide.

And who that wol my jugement withsay,
Shal pay for alle we spenden by the way.
And if ye vouchesauf that it be so,
Telle me anon withouten wordes mo,
And I wol erly shapen me therfore.

This thing was granted, and our othes swore
With ful glad herte, and praiden him also,
That he wold vouchesauf for to don so,
And that he wolde ben our governour,
And of our tales juge and reportour,
And sette a souper at a certain pris;
And we wol reuled ben at his devise,
In highe and lowe : and thus by on assent,
We ben accorded to his jugement.
And therupon the win was fette anon.
We dronken, and to reste wenten eche on,
Withouten any lenger tarying.

A-morwe whan the day began to spring,
Up rose our hoste, and was our aller cok,
And gaderd us togeder in a flok,
And forth we riden a litel more than pas,
Unto the watering of Seint Thomas :
And ther our hoste began his hors arest,
And saide ; lordes, herkeneth if you lest.
Ye wete your forword, and I it record.
If even-song and morwe-song accord,
Let se now who shal telle the first tale.
As ever mote I drinken win or ale,
Who so is rebel to my jugement,
Shal pay for alle that by the way is spent.
Now draweth cutte, or that ye forther twinne.
He which that hath the shortest shal beginne.

Sire knight, (quod he) my maister and my
Now draweth cutte, for that is min accord. [lord,

Cometh nere, (quod he) my lady prioresse,
And ye, sire clerk, let be your shamefastnesse,
Ne studieth nought; lay hand to, every man.

    Anon to drawen every wight began,
And shortly for to tellen as it was,
Were it by aventure, or sort, or cas,
The sothe is this, the cutte felle on the knight,
Of which ful blith and glad was every wight;
And tell he must his tale as was reson,
But forword, and by composition,
As ye han herd; what nedeth wordes mo?
And whan this good man saw that it was so,
As he that wise was and obedient
To kepe his forword by his free assent,
He saide; sithen I shal begin this game,
What? welcome be the cutte a goddes name.
Now let us ride, and herkeneth what I say.

    And with that word we riden forth our way;
And he began with right a mery chere
His tale anon, and saide as ye shul here.

The Knightes Tale.

WHILOM, as olde stories tellen us,
    Ther was a duk that highte Theseus.
Of Athenes he was lord and governour,
And in his time swiche a conquerour,
That greter was ther non under the sonne.
Ful many a riche contree had he wonne.
What with his wisdom and his chevalrie,
He conquerd all the regne of Feminie,

That whilom was ycleped Scythia;
And wedded the fresshe quene Ipolita,
And brought hire home with him to his contree
With mochel glorie and gret solempnitee,
And eke hire yonge suster Emelie.
And thus with victorie and with melodie
Let I this worthy duk to Athenes ride,
And all his host, in armes him beside.

And certes, if it n'ere to long to here,
I wolde have told you fully the manere,
How wonnen was the regne of Feminie,
By Theseus, and by his chevalrie;
And of the grete bataille for the nones
Betwix Athenes and the Amasones;
And how asseged was Ipolita
The faire hardy quene of Scythia;
And of the feste, that was at hire wedding,
And of the temple at hire home coming.
But all this thing I moste as now forbere.
I have, God wot, a large feld to ere;
And weke ben the oxen in my plow.
The remenant of my tale is long ynow.
I wil not letten eke non of this route.
Let every felaw telle his tale aboute,
And let se now who shal the souper winne.
Ther as I left, I wil agen beginne.

This duk, of whom I made mentioun,
Whan he was comen almost to the toun,
In all his wele and in his moste pride,
He was ware, as he cast his eye aside,
Wher that ther kneled in the highe wey
A compagnie of ladies, twey and twey,
Eche after other, clad in clothes blake:
But swiche a crie and swiche a wo they make,

That in this world n'is creature living,
That ever herd swiche another waimenting.
And of this crie ne wolde they never stenten,
Till they the reines of his bridel henten.

What folk be ye that at min home coming
Perturben so my feste with crying?
Quod Theseus; have ye so grete envie
Of min honour, that thus complaine and crie?
Or who hath you misboden, or offended?
Do telle me, if that it may be amended;
And why ye be thus clothed alle in blake?

The oldest lady of hem all than spake,
Whan she had swouned, with a dedly chere,
That it was reuthe for to seen and here.
She sayde; lord, to whom fortune hath yeven
Victorie, and as a conquerour to liven,
Nought greveth us your glorie and your honour;
But we beseke you of mercie and socour.
Have mercie on our woe and our distresse.
Som drope of pitee, thurgh thy gentillesse,
Upon us wretched wimmen let now falle.
For certes, lord, ther n'is non of us alle,
That she n'hath ben a duchesse or a quene;
Now be we caitives, as it is wel sene:
Thanked be fortune, and hire false whele,
That non estat ensureth to be wele.
And certes, lord, to abiden your presence
Here in this temple of the goddesse Clemence
We han ben waiting all this fourtenight:
Now helpe us, lord, sin it lieth in thy might.

I wretched wight, that wepe and waile thus,
Was whilom wif to king Capaneus,
That starfe at Thebes, cursed be that day:
And alle we that ben in this aray,

And maken all this lamentation,
We losten alle our husbondes at that toun,
While that the sege therabouten lay.
And yet now the olde Creon, wala wa!
That lord is now of Thebes the citee,
Fulfilled of ire and of iniquitee,
He for despit, and for his tyrannie,
To don the ded bodies a vilanie,
Of alle our lordes, which that ben yslawe,
Hath alle the bodies on an hepe ydrawe,
And will not suffren hem by non assent
Neyther to ben yberied, ne ybrent,
But maketh houndes ete hem in despite.

And with that word, withouten more respite
They fallen groff, and crien pitously;
Have on us wretched wimmen som mercy,
And let our sorwe sinken in thin herte.

This gentil duk doun from his courser sterte
With herte pitous, whan he herd hem speke.
Him thoughte that his herte wolde all to-breke,
Whan he saw hem so pitous and so mate,
That whilom weren of so gret estate.
And in his armes he hem all up hente,
And hem comforted in ful good entente,
And swore his oth, as he was trewe knight,
He wolde don so ferforthly his might
Upon the tyrant Creon hem to wreke,
That all the peple of Grece shulde speke,
How Creon was of Theseus yserved,
As he that hath his deth ful wel deserved.

And right anon withouten more abode
His banner he displaide, and forth he rode
To Thebes ward, and all his host beside:
No nere Athenes n'olde he go ne ride,

Ne take his ese fully half a day,
But onward on his way that night he lay:
And sent anon Ipolita the quene,
And Emelie hire yonge sister shene
Unto the toun of Athenes for to dwell:
And forth he rit; ther n'is no more to tell.

The red statue of Mars with spere and targe
So shineth in his white banner large,
That all the feldes gliteren up and doun:
And by his banner borne is his penon
Of gold ful riche, in which ther was ybete
The Minotaure which that he slew in Crete.
Thus rit this duk, thus rit this conquerour,
And in his host of chevalrie the flour,
Til that he came to Thebes, and alight
Fayre in a feld, ther as he thought to fight.
But shortly for to speken of this thing,
With Creon, which that was of Thebes king,
He fought, and slew him manly as a knight
In plaine bataille, and put his folk to flight:
And by assaut he wan the citee after,
And rent adoun bothe wall and sparre, and rafter;
And to the ladies he restored again
The bodies of hir housbondes that were slain,
To don the obsequies, as was tho the gise.

But it were all to long for to devise
The grete clamour, and the waimenting,
Whiche that the ladies made at the brenning
Of the bodies, and the gret honour,
That Theseus the noble conquerour
Doth to the ladies, whan they from him wente:
But shortly for to telle is min entente.

Whan that this worthy duk, this Theseus,
Hath Creon slaine, and wonnen Thebes thus,

Still in the feld he toke all night his reste,
And did with all the contree as him leste.
To ransake in the tas of bodies dede,
Hem for to stripe of harneis and of wede,
The pillours dide hir besinesse and cure,
After the bataille and discomfiture.
And so befell, that in the tas they found,
Thurgh girt with many a grevous blody wound,
Two yonge knightes ligging by and by,
Bothe in on armes, wrought ful richely:
Of whiche two, Arcita highte that on,
And he that other highte Palamon.
Not fully quik, ne fully ded they were,
But by hir cote-armure, and by hir gere,
The heraudes knew hem wel in special,
As tho that weren of the blod real
Of Thebes, and of sustren two yborne.
Out of the tas the pillours han hem torne,
And han hem caried soft unto the tente
Of Theseus, and he ful sone hem sente
To Athenes, for to dwellen in prison
Perpetuel, he n'olde no raunson.
And whan this worthy duk had thus ydon,
He toke his host, and home he rit anon
With laurer crouned as a conquerour;
And ther he liveth in joye and in honour
Terme of his lif; what nedeth wordes mo?
And in a tour, in anguish and in wo,
Dwellen this Palamon and eke Arcite,
For evermo, ther may no gold hem quite.

 Thus passeth yere by yere, and day by day,
Till it felle ones in a morwe of May
That Emelie, that fayrer was to sene
Than is the lilie upon his stalke grene,

And fressher than the May with floures newe,
(For with the rose colour strof hire hewe;
I n'ot which was the finer of hem two)
Er it was day, as she was wont to do,
She was arisen, and all redy dight.
For May wol have no slogardie a-night.
The seson priketh every gentil herte,
And maketh him out of his slepe to sterte,
And sayth, arise, and do thin observance.

This maketh Emelie han remembrance
To don honour to May, and for to rise.
Yclothed was she fresshe for to devise.
Hire yelwe here was broided in a tresse,
Behind hire back, a yerde long I gesse.
And in the gardin at the sonne uprist
She walketh up and doun wher as hire list.
She gathereth floures, partie white and red,
To make a sotel gerlond for hire hed,
And as an angel hevenlich she song.
The grete tour, that was so thikke and strong,
Which of the castel was the chef dongeon,
(Wher as these knightes weren in prison,
Of which I tolde you, and tellen shal)
Was even joinant to the gardin wall,
Ther as this Emelie had hire playing.

Bright was the sonne, and clere that morwening,
And Palamon, this woful prisoner,
As was his wone, by leve of his gayler
Was risen, and romed in a chambre on high,
In which he all the noble citee sigh,
And eke the gardin, ful of branches grene,
Ther as this fresshe Emelia the shene
Was in hire walk, and romed up and doun.

This sorweful prisoner, this Palamon

Goth in his chambre roming to and fro,
And to himselfe complaining of his wo:
That he was borne, ful oft he sayd, alas!

And so befell, by aventure or cas,
That thurgh a window thikke of many a barre
Of yren gret, and square as any sparre,
He cast his eyen upon Emelia,
And therwithal he blent and cried, a!
As though he stongen were unto the herte.

And with that crie Arcite anon up sterte,
And saide, cosin min, what eyleth thee,
That art so pale and dedly for to see?
Why cridest thou? who hath thee don offence?
For goddes love, take all in patience
Our prison, for it may non other be.
Fortune hath yeven us this adversite.
Som wikke aspect or disposition
Of Saturne, by som constellation,
Hath yeven us this, although we had it sworn,
So stood the heven whan that we were born,
We moste endure: this is the short and plain.

This Palamon answerde, and sayde again;
Cosin, forsoth of this opinion
Thou hast a vaine imagination.
This prison caused me not for to crie.
But I was hurt right now thurghout min eye
Into min herte, that wol my bane be.
The fayrnesse of a lady that I se
Yond in the gardin roming to and fro,
Is cause of all my crying and my wo.
I n'ot whe'r she be woman or goddesse.
But Venus is it, sothly, as I gesse.

And therwithall on knees adoun he fill,
And sayde: Venus, if it be your will

1   D

You in this gardin thus to transfigure,
Beforn me sorweful wretched creature,
Out of this prison helpe that we may scape.
And if so be our destinee be shape
By eterne word to dien in prison,
Of our lignage have som compassion,
That is so low ybrought by tyrannie.

    And with that word Arcita gan espie
Wher as this lady romed to and fro.
And with that sight hire beautee hurt him so,
That if that Palamon were wounded sore,
Arcite is hurt as moche as he, or more.
And with a sigh he sayde pitously:
The fresshe beautee sleth me sodenly
Of hire that rometh in the yonder place.
And but I have hire mercie and hire grace,
That I may seen hire at the leste way,
I n'am but ded; ther n'is no more to say.

    This Palamon, whan he these wordes herd,
Dispitously he loked, and answerd:
Whether sayest thou this in ernest or in play?

    Nay, quod Arcite, in ernest by my fay.
God helpe me so, me lust full yvel pley.

    This Palamon gan knit his browes twey.
It were, quod he, to thee no gret honour
For to be false, ne for to be traytour
To me, that am thy cosin and thy brother
Ysworne ful depe, and eche of us to other,
That never for to dien in the peine,
Til that the deth departen shal us tweine,
Neyther of us in love to hindre other,
Ne in non other cas, my leve brother;
But that thou shuldest trewely forther me
In every cas, as I shuld forther thee.

This was thin oth, and min also certain ;
I wot it wel, thou darst it not withsain.
Thus art thou of my conseil out of doute.
And now thou woldest falsly ben aboute
To love my lady, whom I love and serve,
And ever shal, til that min herte sterve.

Now certes, false Arcite, thou shalt not so.
I loved hire firste, and tolde thee my wo
As to my conseil, and my brother sworne
To forther me, as I have told beforne.
For which thou art ybounden as a knight
To helpen me, if it lie in thy might,
Or elles art thou false, I dare wel sain.

This Arcita full proudly spake again.
Thou shalt, quod he, be rather false than I.
And thou art false, I tell thee utterly.
For *par amour* I loved hire first or thou.
What wolt thou sayn ? thou wisted nat right now
Whether she were a woman or a goddesse.
Thin is affection of holinesse,
And min is love, as to a creature :
For which I tolde thee min aventure
As to my cosin, and my brother sworne.

I pose, that thou lovedest hire beforne :
Wost thou not wel the olde clerkes sawe,
That who shall give a lover any lawe ?
Love is a greter lawe (by my pan)
Then may be yeven of any erthly man :
And therfore positif lawe, and swiche decree
Is broken all day for love in eche degree.
A man moste nedes love maugre his hed.
He may not fleen it, though he shuld be ded,
All be she maid, or widewe, or elles wif.

And eke it is not likely all thy lif

To stonden in hire grace, no more shal I :
For wel thou wost thyselven veraily,
That thou and I be damned to prison
Perpetuel, us gaineth no raunson.

We strive, as did the houndes for the bone,
They fought all day, and yet hir part was none :
Ther came a kyte, while that they were so wrothe,
And bare away the bone betwix hem bothe.
And therfore at the kinges court, my brother,
Eche man for himself, ther is non other.
Love if thee lust; for I love and ay shal :
And sothly, leve brother, this is al.
Here in this prison mosten we endure,
And everich of us take his aventure.

Gret was the strif, and long betwix hem twey,
If that I hadde leiser for to sey :
But to th' effect. It happed on a day,
(To tell it you as shortly as I may)
A worthy duk that highte Perithous,
That felaw was to this duk Theseus
Sin thilke day that they were children lite,
Was come to Athenes, his felaw to visite,
And for to play, as he was wont to do,
For in this world he loved no man so :
And he loved him as tendrely again.
So wel they loved, as olde bokes sain,
That whan that on was ded, sothly to telle,
His felaw wente and sought him doun in helle :
But of that storie list me not to write.

Duk Perithous loved wel Arcite,
And had him knowe at Thebes yere by yere :
And finally at request and praiere
Of Perithous, withouten any raunson
Duk Theseus him let out of prison,

Frely to gon, wher that him list over all,
In swiche a gise, as I you tellen shall.

This was the forword, plainly for to endite,
Betwixen Theseus and him Arcite:
That if so were, that Arcite were yfound
Ever in his lif, by day or night, o stound
In any contree of this Theseus,
And he were caught, it was accorded thus,
That with a swerd he shulde lese his hed;
Ther was non other remedie ne rede.
But taketh his leve, and homeward he him spedde;
Let him beware, his nekke lieth to wedde.

How gret a sorwe suffereth now Arcite?
The deth he feleth thurgh his herte smite;
He wepeth, waileth, crieth pitously;
To sleen himself he waiteth prively.
He said; Alas the day that I was borne!
Now is my prison werse than beforne:
Now is me shape eternally to dwelle
Not only in purgatorie, but in helle.
Alas! that ever I knew Perithous.
For elles had I dwelt with Theseus
Yfetered in his prison evermo.
Than had I ben in blisse, and not in wo.
Only the sight of hire, whom that I serve,
Though that I never hire grace may deserve,
Wold have sufficed right ynough for me.

O dere cosin Palamon, quod he,
Thin is the victorie of this aventure.
Ful blisful in prison maiest thou endure:
In prison? certes nay, but in paradise.
Wel hath fortune yturned thee the dise,
That hast the sight of hire, and I th' absence.
For possible is, sin thou hast hire presence,

And art a knight, a worthy and an able,
That by som cas, sin fortune is changeable,
Thou maiest to thy desir somtime atteine.
But I that am exiled, and barreine
Of alle grace, and in so gret despaire,
That ther n'is erthe, water, fire, ne aire,
Ne creature, that of hem maked is,
That may me hele, or don comfort in this,
Wel ought I sterve in wanhope and distresse.
Farewel my lif, my lust, and my gladnesse.

 Alas, why plainen men so in commune
Of purveyance of God, or of fortune,
That yeveth hem ful oft in many a gise
Wel better than they can hemself devise?
Som man desireth for to have richesse,
That cause is of his murdre or gret siknesse.
And som man wold out of his prison fayn,
That in his house is of his meinie slain.
Infinite harmes ben in this matere.
We wote not what thing that we praien here.
We faren as he that dronke is as a mous.
A dronken man wot wel he hath an hous,
But he ne wot which is the right way thider,
And to a dronken man the way is slider.
And certes in this world so faren we.

 We seken fast after felicite,
But we go wrong ful often trewely.
Thus we may sayen alle, and namely I,
That wende, and had a gret opinion,
That if I might escapen fro prison
Than had I ben in joye and parfite hele,
Ther now I am exiled fro my wele.
Sin that I may not seen you, Emelie,
I n'am but ded ; ther n'is no remedie.

Upon that other side Palamon,
Whan that he wist Arcita was agon,
Swiche sorwe he maketh, that the grete tour
Resouned of his yelling and clamour.
The pure fetters on his shinnes grete
Were of his bitter salte teres wete.

Alas! quod he, Arcita cosin min,
Of all our strif, God wot, the frute is thin.
Thou walkest now in Thebes at thy large,
And of my wo thou yevest litel charge.
Thou maist, sith thou hast wisdom and manhede,
Assemblen all the folk of our kinrede,
And make a werre so sharpe on this contree,
That by som aventure, or som tretee,
Thou maist have hire to lady and to wif,
For whom that I must nedes lese my lif.
For as by way of possibilitee,
Sith thou art at thy large of prison free,
And art a lord, gret is thin avantage,
More than is min, that sterve here in a cage.
For I may wepe and waile, while that I live,
With all the wo that prison may me yeve,
And eke with peine that love me yeveth also,
That doubleth all my tourment and my wo.

Therwith the fire of jalousie up sterte
Within his brest, and hent him by the herte
So woodly, that he like was to behold
The box-tree, or the ashen ded and cold.
Than said he; O cruel goddes, that governe
This world with binding of your word eterne,
And writen in the table of athamant
Your parlement and your eterne grant,
What is mankind more unto you yhold
Than is the shepe, that rouketh in the fold?

For slain is man, right as another beest,
And dwelleth eke in prison, and arrest,
And hath siknesse, and gret adversite,
And oftentimes gilteles parde.

What governance is in this prescience,
That gilteles turmenteth innocence?
And yet encreseth this all my penance,
That man is bounden to his observance
For Goddes sake to leten of his will,
Ther as a beest may all his lust fulfill.
And whan a beest is ded, he hath no peine;
But man after his deth mote wepe and pleine,
Though in this world he have care and wo:
Withouten doute it maye stonden so.

The answer of this lete I to divines,
But wel I wote, that in this world gret pine is.
Alas! I see a serpent or a thefe,
That many a trewe man hath do meschefe,
Gon at his large, and wher him lust may turn.
But I moste ben in prison thurgh Saturn,
And eke thurgh Juno, jalous and eke wood,
That hath wel neye destruied all the blood
Of Thebes, with his waste walles wide.
And Venus sleeth me on that other side
For jalousie, and fere of him Arcite.

Now wol I stent of Palamon a lite,
And leten him in his prison still dwelle,
And of Arcita forth I wol you telle.

The sommer passeth, and the nightes long
Encresen double wise the peines strong
Both of the lover, and of the prisoner.
I n'ot which hath the wofuller mistere.
For, shortly for to say, this Palamon
Perpetuelly is damned to prison,

In chaines and in fetters to ben ded;
And Arcite is exiled on his hed
For evermore as out of that contree,
Ne never more he shal his lady see.

You lovers axe I now this question,
Who hath the werse, Arcite or Palamon?
That on may se his lady day by day,
But in prison moste he dwellen alway.
That other wher him lust may ride or go,
But sen his lady shal he never mo.
Now demeth as you liste, ye that can,
For I wol tell you forth as I began.

Whan that Arcite to Thebes comen was,
Ful oft a day he swelt and said alas,
For sen his lady shal he never mo.
And shortly to concluden all his wo,
So mochel sorwe hadde never creature,
That is or shal be, while the world may dure.
His slepe, his mete, his drinke is him byraft,
That lene he wex, and drie as is a shaft.
His eyen holwe, and grisly to behold,
His hewe falwe, and pale as ashen cold,
And solitary he was, and ever alone,
And wailing all the night, making his mone.
And if he herde song or instrument,
Than wold he wepe, he mighte not be stent.
So feble were his spirites, and so low,
And changed so, that no man coude know
His speche ne his vois, though men it herd.
And in his gere, for all the world he ferd
Nought only like the lovers maladie
Of Ereos, but rather ylike manie,
Engendred of humours melancolike,
Beforne his hed in his celle fantastike.

And shortly turned was all up so doun
Both habit and eke dispositioun
Of him, this woful lover dan Arcite.
What shuld I all day of his wo endite?

Whan he endured had a yere or two
This cruel torment, and this peine and wo,
At Thebes, in his contree, as I said,
Upon a night in slepe as he him laid,
Him thought how that the winged god Mercury
Beforne him stood, and bad him to be mery.
His slepy yerde in hond he bare upright;
An hat he wered upon his heres bright.
Arraied was this god (as he toke kepe)
As he was whan that Argus toke his slepe;
And said him thus: To Athenes shalt thou
Ther is thee shapen of thy wo an ende. [wende;

And with that word Arcite awoke and stert.
Now trewely how sore that ever me smert,
Quod he, to Athenes right now wol I fare.
Ne for no drede of deth shal I not spare
To se my lady, that I love and serve;
In hire presence I rekke not to sterve.
And with that word he caught a gret mirrour,
And saw that changed was all his colour,
And saw his visage all in another kind.
And right anon it ran him in his mind,
That sith his face was so disfigured
Of maladie the which he had endured,
He mighte wel, if that he bare him lowe,
Live in Athenes evermore unknowe,
And sen his lady wel nigh day by day.
And right anon he changed his aray,
And clad him as a poure labourer.
And all alone, save only a squier,

That knew his privitee and all his cas,
Which was disguised pourely as he was,
To Athenes is he gon the nexte way.
And to the court he went upon a day,
And at the gate he proffered his service,
To drugge and draw, what so men wold devise.
And shortly of this matere for to sayn,
He fell in office with a chamberlain,
The which that dwelling was with Emelie.
For he was wise, and coude sone espie
Of every servant, which that served hire.
Wel coude he hewen wood, and water bere,
For he was yonge and mighty for the nones,
And therto he was strong and big of bones
To don that any wight can him devise.
　　A yere or two he was in this service,
Page of the chambre of Emelie the bright;
And Philostrate he sayde that he hight.
But half so wel beloved a man as he,
Ne was ther never in court of his degre.
He was so gentil of conditioun,
That thurghout all the court was his renoun.
They sayden that it were a charite
That Theseus wold enhaunsen his degre,
And putten him in worshipful service,
Ther as he might his vertues exercise.
And thus within a while his name is spronge
Both of his dedes, and of his good tonge,
That Theseus hath taken him so ner
That of his chambre he made him a squier,
And gave him gold to mainteine his degre;
And eke men brought him out of his contre
Fro yere to yere ful prively his rent.
But honestly and sleighly he it spent,

That no man wondred how that he it hadde.
And thre yere in this wise his lif he ladde,
And bare him so in pees and eke in werre,
Ther n'as no man that Theseus hath derre.
And in this blisse let I now Arcite,
And speke I wol of Palamon a lite.

In derkenesse and horrible and strong prison
This seven yere hath sitten Palamon,
Forpined, what for love and for distresse.
Who feleth double sorwe and hevinesse
But Palamon? that love distraineth so,
That wood out of his wit he goth for wo,
And eke therto he is a prisonere
Perpetuell, not only for a yere.

Who coude rime in English proprely
His martirdom? forsoth it am not I,
Therfore I passe as lightly as I may.
It fell that in the seventh yere in May
The thridde night, (as olde bokes sayn,
That all this storie tellen more plain)
Were it by aventure or destinee,
(As, whan a thing is shapen, it shal be,)
That sone after the midnight, Palamon
By helping of a frend brake his prison,
And fleeth the cite faste as he may go,
For he had yeven drinke his gayler so
Of a clarre, made of a certain wine,
With narcotikes and opie of Thebes fine,
That all the night though that men wold him shake,
The gailer slept, he mighte not awake.
And thus he fleeth as faste as ever he may.

The night was short, and faste by the day,
That nedes cost he moste himselven hide.
And to a grove faste ther beside

With dredful foot than stalketh Palamon.
For shortly this was his opinion,
That in that grove he wold him hide all day,
And in the night than wold he take his way
To Thebes ward, his frendes for to preie
On Theseus to helpen him werreie.
And shortly, eyther he wold lese his lif,
Or winnen Emelie unto his wif.
This is the effect, and his entente plein.

    Now wol I turnen to Arcite agein,
That litel wist how neighe was his care,
Til that fortune had brought him in the snare.
The besy larke, the messager of day,
Saleweth in hire song the morwe gray;
And firy Phebus riseth up so bright,
That all the orient laugheth of the sight,
And with his stremes drieth in the greves
The silver dropes, hanging on the leves,
And Arcite, that is in the court real
With Theseus the squier principal,
Is risen, and loketh on the mery day.
And for to don his observance to May,
Remembring on the point of his desire,
He on his courser, sterting as the fire,
Is ridden to the feldes him to pley,
Out of the court, were it a mile or twey.
And to the grove of which that I you told,
By aventure his way he gan to hold,
To maken him a gerlond of the greves,
Were it of woodbind or of hauthorn leves,
And loud he song agen the sonne shene.

    O Maye, with all thy floures and thy grene,
Right welcome be thou faire freshe May,
I hope that I some grene here getten may.

And from his courser, with a lusty herte
Into the grove ful hastily he sterte,
And in a path he romed up and doun,
Ther as by aventure this Palamon
Was in a bush, that no man might him se,
For sore afered of his deth was he.
Nothing ne knew he that it was Arcite.
God wot he wold have trowed it ful lite.
But soth is said, gon sithen are many yeres,
That feld hath eyen, and the wood hath eres.
It is ful faire a man to bere him even,
For al day meten men at unset steven.
Ful litel wote Arcite of his felaw,
That was so neigh to herken of his saw,
For in the bush he sitteth now ful still.

    Whan that Arcite had romed all his fill,
And songen all the roundel lustily,
Into a studie he fell sodenly,
As don these lovers in hir queinte geres,
Now in the crop, and now doun in the breres,
Now up, now doun, as boket in a well.
Right as the Friday, sothly for to tell,
Now shineth it, and now it raineth fast,
Right so can gery Venus overcast
The hertes of hire folk, right as hire day
Is gerfull, right so changeth she aray.
Selde is the Friday all the weke ylike.

    Whan Arcite hadde ysonge, he gan to sike,
And set him doun withouten any more:
Alas! (quod he) the day that I was bore!
How longe, Juno, thurgh thy crueltee
Wilt thou werreien Thebes the citee?
Alas! ybrought is to confusion
The blood real of Cadme and Amphion:

Of Cadmus, which that was the firste man,
That Thebes built, or firste the toun began,
And of the citee firste was crouned king.
Of his linage am I, and his ofspring
By veray line, as of the stok real:
And now I am so caitif and so thral,
That he that is my mortal enemy,
I serve him as his squier pourely.
And yet doth Juno me wel more shame,
For I dare not beknowe min owen name,
But ther as I was wont to highte Arcite,
Now highte I Philostrat, not worth a mite.
Alas! thou fell Mars, alas! thou Juno,
Thus hath your ire our linage all fordo,
Save only me, and wretched Palamon,
That Theseus martireth in prison.
And over all this, to slen me utterly,
Love hath his firy dart so brenningly
Ystiked thurgh my trewe careful hert,
That shapen was my deth erst than my shert.
Ye slen me with your eyen, Emelie;
Ye ben the cause wherfore that I die.
Of all the remenant of min other care
Ne set I not the mountance of a tare,
So that I coud don ought to your plesance.

And with that word he fell doun in a trance
A longe time; and afterward up sterte
This Palamon, that thought thurghout his herte
He felt a colde swerd sodenly glide:
For ire he quoke, no lenger wolde he hide.
And whan that he had herd Arcites tale,
As he were wood, with face ded and pale,
He sterte him up out of the bushes thikke,
And sayde: False Arcite, false traitour wicke,

Now art thou hent, that lovest my lady so,
For whom that I have all this peine and wo,
And art my blood, and to my conseil sworn,
As I ful oft have told thee herebeforn,
And hast bejaped here duk Theseus,
And falsely changed hast thy name thus:
I wol be ded, or elles thou shalt die.
Thou shalt not love my lady Emelie,
But I wol love hire only and no mo.
For I am Palamon thy mortal fo.
And though that I no wepen have in this place,
But out of prison am astert by grace,
I drede nought, that eyther thou shalt die,
Or thou ne shalt nat loven Emelie.
Chese which thou wolt, for thou shalt not asterte.

This Arcite tho, with ful dispitous herte,
Whan he him knew, and had his tale herd,
As fers as a leon, pulled out a swerd,
And sayde thus; By God that sitteth above,
N'ere it that thou art sike, and wood for love,
And eke that thou no wepen hast in this place,
Thou shuldest never out of this grove pace,
That thou ne shuldest dien of min hond.
For I defie the suretee and the bond,
Which that thou saist that I have made to thee.
What? veray fool, thinke wel that love is free,
And I wol love hire maugre all thy might.
But, for thou art a worthy gentil knight,
And wilnest to darraine hire by bataille,
Have here my trouth, to-morwe I will not faille,
Withouten weting of any other wight,
That here I wol be founden as a knight,
And bringen harneis right ynough for thee;
And chese the beste, and leve the werste for me.

And mete and drinke this night wol I bring
Ynough for thee, and clothes for thy bedding.
And if so be that thou my lady win,
And sle me in this wode, ther I am in,
Thou maist wel have thy lady as for me.

This Palamon answerd, I grant it thee.
And thus they ben departed til a-morwe,
Whan eche of hem hath laid his faith to borwe.

O Cupide, out of alle charitee!
O regne, that wolt no felaw have with thee!
Ful soth is sayde, that love ne lordship
Wol nat, his thankes, have no felawship.
Wel finden that Arcite and Palamon.

Arcite is ridden anon unto the toun,
And on the morwe, or it were day light,
Ful prively two harneis hath he dight,
Both suffisant and mete to darreine
The bataille in the feld betwix hem tweine.
And on his hors, alone as he was borne,
He carieth all this harneis him beforne;
And in the grove, at time and place ysette,
This Arcite and this Palamon ben mette.
Tho changen gan the colour of hir face.
Right as the hunter in the regne of Trace
That stondeth at a gappe with a spere,
Whan hunted is the lion or the bere,
And hereth him come rushing in the greves,
And breking bothe the boughes and the leves,
And thinketh, here cometh my mortal enemy,
Withouten faille, he must be ded or I;
For eyther I mote slen him at the gappe;
Or he mote slen me, if that me mishappe:
So ferden they, in changing of hir hewe,
As fer as eyther of hem other knewe.

I   E

Ther n'as no good day, ne no saluing.
But streit withouten wordes rehersing,
Everich of hem halpe to armen other,
As frendly, as he were his owen brother.
And after that, with sharpe speres strong
They foineden eche at other wonder long.
Thou mightest wenen, that this Palamon
In his fighting were as a wood leon,
And as a cruel tigre was Arcite :
As wilde bores gan they togeder smite,
That frothen white as fome for ire wood.
Up to the ancle foughte they in hir blood.
And in this wise I let hem fighting dwelle,
And forth I wol of Theseus you telle.

The destinee, ministre general,
That executeth in the world over al
The purveiance, that God hath sen beforne ;
So strong it is, that though the world had sworne
The contrary of a thing by ya, or nay,
Yet somtime it shall fallen on a day
That falleth nat efte in a thousand yere.
For certainly our appetites here,
Be it of werre, or pees, or hate, or love,
All is this ruled by the sight above.
This mene I now by mighty Theseus,
That for to hunten is so desirous,
And namely at the grete hart in May,
That in his bed ther daweth him no day,
That he n'is clad, and redy for to ride
With hunte and horne, and houndes him beside.
For in his hunting hath he swiche delite,
That it is all his joye and appetite
To ben himself the grete hartes bane,
For after Mars he serveth now Diane.

Clere was the day, as I have told or this,
And Theseus, with alle joye and blis,
With his Ipolita, the fayre quene,
And Emelie, yclothed all in grene,
On hunting ben they ridden really.
And to the grove, that stood ther faste by,
In which ther was an hart as men him told,
Duk Theseus the streite way hath hold.
And to the launde he rideth him ful right,
Ther was the hart ywont to have his flight,
And over a brooke, and so forth on his wey.
This duk wol have a cours at him or twey
With houndes, swiche as him lust to commaunde.
And when this duk was comen to the launde,
Under the sonne he loked, and anon
He was ware of Arcite and Palamon,
That foughten breme, as it were bolles two.
The brighte swerdes wenten to and fro
So hidously, that with the leste stroke
It semed that it wolde felle an oke.
But what they weren, nothing he ne wote.
This duk his courser with his sporres smote,
And at a stert he was betwix hem two,
And pulled out a swerd and cried, ho !
No more, up peine of lesing of your hed.
By mighty Mars, he shal anon be ded,
That smiteth any stroke, that I may sen.
But telleth me what mistere men ye ben,
That ben so hardy for to fighten here
Withouten any juge other officere,
As though it were in listes really.

This Palamon answered hastily,
And saide : Sire, what nedeth wordes mo ?
We have the deth deserved bothe two.

Two woful wretches ben we, two caitives,
That ben accombred of our owen lives,
And as thou art a rightful lord and juge,
Ne yeve us neyther mercie ne refuge.
And sle me first, for seinte charitee.
But sle my felaw eke as wel as me.
Or sle him first; for, though thou know it lite,
This is thy mortal fo, this is Arcite,
That fro thy lond is banished on his hed,
For which he hath deserved to be ded.
For this is he that came unto thy gate
And sayde, that he highte Philostrate.
Thus hath he japed thee ful many a yere,
And thou hast maked him thy chief squiere,
And this is he, that loveth Emelie.

For sith the day is come that I shal die
I make plainly my confession,
That I am thilke woful Palamon,
That hath thy prison broken wilfully.
I am thy mortal fo, and it am I
That loveth so hot Emelie the bright,
That I wold dien present in hire sight.
Therfore I axe deth and my jewise.
But sle my felaw in the same wise,
For both we have deserved to be slain.

This worthy duk answerd anon again,
And sayd, This is a short conclusion.
Your owen mouth, by your confession
Hath damned you, and I wol it recorde.
It nedeth not to peine you with the corde.
Ye shul be ded by mighty Mars the rede.

The quene anon for veray womanhede
Gan for to wepe, and so did Emelie,
And all the ladies in the compagnie.

Gret pite was it, as it thought hem alle,
That ever swiche a chance shulde befalle.
For gentil men they were of gret estat,
And nothing but for love was this debat.
And sawe hir blody woundes wide and sore ;
And alle criden bothe lesse and more,
Have mercie, Lord, upon us wimmen alle.
And on hir bare knees adoun they falle,
And wold have kist his feet ther as he stood,
Till at the last, aslaked was his mood ;
(For pitee renneth sone in gentil herte)
And though he first for ire quoke and sterte,
He hath considered shortly in a clause
The trespas of hem both, and eke the cause :
And although that his ire hir gilt accused,
Yet in his reson he hem both excused ;
As thus ; he thoughte wel that every man
Wol helpe himself in love if that he can,
And eke deliver himself out of prison.
And eke his herte had compassion
Of wimmen, for they wepten ever in on :
And in his gentil herte he thoughte anon,
And soft unto himself he sayed : fie
Upon a lord that wol have no mercie,
But be a leon both in word and dede,
To hem that ben in repentance and drede,
As wel as to a proud dispitous man,
That wol mainteinen that he first began.
That lord hath litel of discretion,
That in swiche cas can no division :
But weigheth pride and humblesse after on.
And shortly, whan his ire is thus agon,
He gan to loken up with eyen light,
And spake these same wordes all on hight.

The god of love, a! *benedicite*,
How mighty and how grete a lord is he?
Again his might ther gainen non obstacles,
He may be cleped a God for his miracles.
For he can maken at his owen gise
Of everich herte, as that him list devise.

Lo here this Arcite, and this Palamon,
That quitely weren out of my prison,
And might have lived in Thebes really,
And weten I am hir mortal enemy,
And that hir deth lith in my might also,
And yet hath love, maugre hir eyen two,
Ybrought hem hither bothe for to die.
Now loketh, is not this an heigh folie?
Who maye ben a fool, but if he love?
Behold for Goddes sake that sitteth above,
Se how they blede! be they not wel araied?
Thus hath hir lord, the god of love, hem paied
Hir wages, and hir fees for hir service.
And yet they wenen for to be ful wise,
That serven love, for ought that may befalle.
And yet is this the beste game of alle,
That she, for whom they have this jolite,
Con hem therfore as mochel thank as me.
She wot no more of alle this hote fare
By God, than wot a cuckow or an hare.
But all mote ben assaied, hote or cold;
A man mote ben a fool other yonge or old;
I wot it by myself ful yore agon:
For in my time a servant was I on.
And therfore sith I know of loves peine,
And wot how sore it can a man destreine,
As he that oft hath ben caught in his las,
I you foryeve all holly this trespas,

At request of the quene that kneleth here,
And eke of Emelie, my suster dere.
And ye shul bothe anon unto me swere,
That never mo ye shul my contree dere,
Ne maken werre upon me night ne day,
But ben my frendes in alle that ye may.
I you foryeve this trespas every del.
And they him sware his axing fayr and wel,
And him of lordship and of mercie praid,
And he hem granted grace, and thus he said:

To speke of real linage and richesse,
Though that she were a quene or a princesse,
Eche of you bothe is worthy douteles
To wedden whan time is, but natheles
I speke as for my suster Emelie,
For whom ye have this strif and jalousie,
Ye wot yourself, she may not wedden two
At ones, though ye fighten evermo:
But on of you, al be him loth or lefe,
He mot gon pipen in an ivy lefe:
This is to say, she may not have you bothe,
Al be ye never so jalous, ne so wrothe.
And forthy I you put in this degree,
That eche of you shall have his destinee,
As him is shape, and herkneth in what wise;
Lo here your ende of that I shal devise.

My will is this for plat conclusion
Withouten any replication,
If that you liketh, take it for the beste,
That everich of you shal gon wher him leste
Freely withouten raunson or dangere;
And this day fifty wekes, ferre ne nere,
Everich of you shal bring an hundred knightes,
Armed for listes up at alle rightes

Alle redy to darrein hire by bataille.
And this behete I you withouten faille
Upon my trouth, and as I am a knight,
That whether of you bothe hath that might,
This is to sayn, that whether he or thou
May with his hundred, as I spake of now,
Sle his contrary, or out of listes drive,
Him shall I yeven Emelie to wive,
To whom that fortune yeveth so fayr a grace.

　The listes shal I maken in this place,
And God so wisly on my soule rewe,
As I shal even juge ben, and trewe.
Ye shal non other ende with me maken
That on of you ne shal be ded or taken.
And if you thinketh this is wel ysaid,
Saith your avis, and holdeth you apaid.
This is your ende, and your conclusion.

　Who loketh lightly now but Palamon?
Who springeth up for joye but Arcite?
Who coud it tell, or who coud it endite,
The joye that is maked in the place
Whan Theseus hath don so fayre a grace?
But doun on knees went every manere wight,
And thanked him with all hir hertes might,
And namely these Thebanes often sith.

　And thus with good hope and with herte blith
They taken hir leve, and homeward gan they ride
To Thebes, with his olde walles wide.

　I trowe men wolde deme it negligence,
If I foryete to tellen the dispence
Of Theseus, that goth so besily
To maken up the listes really,
That swiche a noble theatre as it was,
I dare wel sayn, in all this world ther n'as.

The circuite a mile was aboute,
Walled of stone, and diched all withoute.
Round was the shape, in manere of a compas
Ful of degrees, the hight of sixty pas,
That whan a man was set on o degree
He letted not his felaw for to see.
Estward ther stood a gate of marbel white,
Westward right swiche another in th' opposite.
And shortly to concluden, swiche a place
Was never in erthe, in so litel a space,
For in the lond ther n'as no craftes man,
That geometrie, or arsmetrike can,
Ne portreiour, ne kerver of images,
That Theseus ne yaf him mete and wages
The theatre for to maken and devise.

And for to don his rite and sacrifice,
He estward hath upon the gate above,
In worship of Venus goddesse of love,
Don make an auter and an oratorie;
And westward in the minde and in memorie
Of Mars he maked hath right swiche another,
That coste largely of gold a fother.
And northward, in a touret on the wall,
Of alabastre white and red corall
An oratorie riche for to see,
In worship of Diane of chastitee,
Hath Theseus don wrought in noble wise.

But yet had I foryetten to devise
The noble kerving, and the portreitures,
The shape, the contenance of the figures
That weren in these oratories three.

First in the temple of Venus maist thou see
Wrought on the wall, ful pitous to beholde,
The broken slepes, and the sikes colde,

The sacred teres, and the waimentinges,
The firy strokes of the desiringes,
That loves servants in this lif enduren;
The othes, that hir covenants assuren.
Plesance and hope, desire, foolhardinesse,
Beaute and youthe, baudrie and richesse,
Charmes and force, lesinges and flaterie,
Dispence, besinesse, and jalousie,
That wered of yelwe goldes a gerlond,
And hadde a cuckow sitting on hire hond,
Festes, instruments, and caroles and dances,
Lust and array, and all the circumstances
Of love, which that I reken and reken shall,
By ordre weren peinted on the wall,
And mo than I can make of mention.
For sothly all the mount of Citheron,
Ther Venus hath hire principal dwelling,
Was shewed on the wall in purtreying,
With all the gardin, and the lustinesse.
Nought was foryetten the porter idelnesse,
Ne Narcissus the fayre of yore agon,
Ne yet the folie of king Salomon,
Ne yet the grete strengthe of Hercules,
Th' enchantment of Medea and Circes,
Ne of Turnus the hardy fiers corage,
The riche Cresus caitif in servage.
Thus may ye seen, that wisdom ne richesse,
Beaute ne sleighte, strengthe ne hardinesse,
Ne may with Venus holden champartie,
For as hire liste the world may she gie.
Lo, all these folk so caught were in hire las
Til they for wo ful often said alas.
Sufficeth here ensamples on or two,
And yet I coude reken a thousand mo.

The statue of Venus glorious for to see
Was naked fleting in the large see,
And fro the navel doun all covered was
With wawes grene, and bright as any glas.
A citole in hire right hand hadde she,
And on hire hed, ful semely for to see,
A rose gerlond fressh, and wel smelling,
Above hire hed hire doves fleckering.
Before hire stood hire sone Cupido,
Upon his shoulders winges had he two;
And blind he was, as it is often sene;
A bow he bare and arwes bright and kene.

Why shulde I not as wel eke tell you all
The purtreiture, that was upon the wall
Within the temple of mighty Mars the rede?
All peinted was the wall in length and brede
Like to the estres of the grisly place,
That highte the gret temple of Mars in Trace,
In thilke colde and frosty region,
Ther as Mars hath his sovereine mansion.

First on the wall was peinted a forest,
In which ther wonneth neyther man ne best,
With knotty knarry barrein trees old
Of stubbes sharpe and hidous to behold;
In which ther ran a romble and a swough,
As though a storme shuld bresten every bough:
And dounward from an hill under a bent,
Ther stood the temple of Mars armipotent,
Wrought all of burned stele, of which th' entree
Was longe and streite, and gastly for to see.
And therout came a rage and swiche a vise,
That it made all the gates for to rise.
The northern light in at the dore shone,
For window on the wall ne was ther none,

Thurgh which men mighten any light discerne.
The dore was all of athamant eterne,
Yclenched overthwart and endelong
With yren tough, and for to make it strong,
Every piler the temple to sustene
Was tonne-gret, of yren bright and shene.

Ther saw I first the derke imagining
Of felonie, and alle the compassing;
The cruel ire, red as any glede,
The pikepurse, and eke the pale drede;
The smiler with the knif under the cloke,
The shepen brenning with the blake smoke;
The treson of the mordring in the bedde,
The open werre, with woundes all bebledde;
Conteke with blody knif, and sharp manace.
All full of chirking was that sory place.
The sleer of himself yet saw I there,
His herte-blood hath bathed all his here:
The naile ydriven in the shode on hight,
The colde deth, with mouth gaping upright.
Amiddes of the temple sate mischance,
With discomfort and sory contenance.
Yet saw I woodnesse laughing in his rage,
Armed complaint, outhees, and fiers outrage;
The carraine in the bush, with throte ycorven,
A thousand slain, and not of qualme ystorven;
The tirant, with the prey by force yraft;
The toun destroied, ther was nothing laft.
Yet saw I brent the shippes hoppesteres,
The hunte ystrangled with the wilde beres:
The sow freting the child right in the cradel;
The coke yscalled, for all his long ladel.
Nought was foryete by th' infortune of Marte
The carter overridden with his carte;

Under the wheel ful low he lay adoun.
  Ther were also of Martes division,
Th' armerer, and the bowyer, and the smith,
That forgeth sharpe swerdes on his stith.
And all above depeinted in a tour
Saw I conquest, sitting in gret honour,
With thilke sharpe swerd over his hed
Yhanging by a subtil twined thred.
Depeinted was the slaughter of Julius,
Of gret Nero, and of Antonius:
All be that thilke time they were unborne,
Yet was hir deth depeinted therbeforne,
By manacing of Mars, right by figure,
So was it shewed in that purtreiture
As is depeinted in the cercles above,
Who shal be slaine or elles ded for love.
Sufficeth on ensample in stories olde,
I may not reken hem alle, though I wolde.
  The statue of Mars upon a carte stood
Armed, and loked grim as he were wood,
And over his hed ther shinen two figures
Of sterres, that ben cleped in scriptures,
That on Puella, that other Rubeus.
This God of armes was araied thus:
A wolf ther stood before him at his fete
With eyen red, and of a man he ete:
With subtil pensil peinted was this storie,
In redouting of Mars and of his glorie.
  Now to the temple of Diane the chaste
As shortly as I can I wol me haste,
To tellen you of the descriptioun,
Depeinted by the walles up and doun,
Of hunting and of shamefast chastitee.
Ther saw I how woful Calistope,

Whan that Diane agreved was with here,
Was turned from a woman til a bere,
And after was she made the lodesterre:
Thus was it peinted, I can say no ferre;
Hire sone is eke a sterre as men may see.
Ther saw I Dane yturned til a tree,
I mene not hire the goddesse Diane,
But Peneus daughter, which that highte Dane.
Ther saw I Atteon an hart ymaked,
For vengeance that he saw Diane all naked:
I saw how that his houndes have him caught,
And freten him, for that they knew him naught.
Yet peinted was a litel forthermore,
How Athalante hunted the wilde bore,
And Meleagre, and many another mo,
For which Diane wroughte hem care and wo.
Ther saw I many another wonder storie,
The which me liste not drawen to memorie.

This goddesse on an hart ful heye sete,
With smale houndes all aboute hire fete,
And undernethe hire feet she hadde a mone,
Wexing it was, and shulde wanen sone.
In gaudy grene hire statue clothed was,
With bow in hond, and arwes in a cas.
Hire eyen caste she ful low adoun,
Ther Pluto hath his derke regioun.
A woman travailling was hire beforne,
But for hire childe so longe was unborne
Ful pitously Lucina gan she call,
And sayed; helpe, for thou mayst beste of all.
Wel coude he peinten lifly that it wrought,
With many a florein he the hewes bought.

Now ben these listes made, and Theseus
That at his grete cost arraied thus

The temples, and the theatre everidel,
Whan it was don, him liked wonder wel.
But stint I wol of Theseus a lite,
And speke of Palamon and of Arcite.

The day approcheth of hir returning,
That everich shuld an hundred knightes bring,
The bataille to darreine, as I you told ;
And til Athenes, hir covenant for to hold,
Hath everich of hem brought an hundred
      knightes,
Wel armed for the werre at alle rightes.
And sikerly ther trowed many a man,
That never, sithen that the world began,
As for to speke of knighthood of hir hond,
As fer as God hath maked see and lond,
N'as, of so fewe, so noble a compagnie.
For every wight that loved chevalrie,
And wold, his thankes, han a passant name,
Hath praied, that he might ben of that game,
And wel was him, that therto chosen was.
For if ther fell to-morwe swiche a cas,
Ye knowen wel, that every lusty knight,
That loveth *par amour*, and hath his might,
Were it in Englelond, or elleswher,
They wold, hir thankes, willen to be ther.
To fight for a lady, a ! *benedicite*,
It were a lusty sighte for to se.

And right so ferden they with Palamon.
With him ther wenten knightes many on.
Som wol ben armed in an habergeon,
And in a brest plate, and in a gipon ;
And som wol have a pair of plates large ;
And som wol have a Pruce sheld, or a targe ;
Som wol ben armed on his legges wele,

And have an axe, and som a mace of stele.
Ther n'is no newe guise, that it n'as old.
Armed they weren, as I have you told,
Everich after his opinion.

Ther maist thou se coming with Palamon
Licurge himself, the grete king of Trace:
Blake was his berd, and manly was his face.
The cercles of his eyen in his hed
They gloweden betwixen yelwe and red,
And like a griffon loked he about,
With kemped heres on his browes stout;
His limmes gret, his braunes hard and stronge,
His shouldres brode, his armes round and longe.
And as the guise was in his contree,
Ful highe upon a char of gold stood he,
With foure white bolles in the trais.
Instede of cote-armure on his harnais,
With nayles yelwe, and bright as any gold,
He hadde a beres skin, cole-blake for old.
His longe here was kempt behind his bak,
As any ravenes fether it shone for blake.
A wreth of gold arm-gret, of huge weight,
Upon his hed sate ful of stones bright,
Of fine rubins and of diamants.
About his char ther wenten white alauns,
Twenty and mo, as gret as any stere,
To hunten at the leon or the dere,
And folwed him, with mosel fast ybound,
Colered with gold, and torettes filed round.
An hundred lordes had he in his route
Armed full wel, with hertes sterne and stoute.

With Arcita, in stories as men find,
The gret Emetrius the king of Inde,
Upon a stede bay, trapped in stele,

Covered with cloth of gold diapred wele,
Came riding like the god of armes Mars.
His cote-armure was of a cloth of Tars,
Couched with perles, white, and round and grete.
His sadel was of brent gold new ybete;
A mantelet upon his shouldres hanging
Bret-ful of rubies red, as fire sparkling.
His crispe here like ringes was yronne,
And that was yelwe, and glitered as the sonne.
His nose was high, his eyen bright citrin,
His lippes round, his colour was sanguin,
A fewe fraknes in his face yspreint,
Betwixen yelwe and blake somdel ymeint,
And as a leon he his loking caste.
Of five and twenty yere his age I caste.
His berd was wel begonnen for to spring;
His vois was as a trompe thondering.
Upon his hed he wered of laurer grene
A gerlond fresshe and lusty for to sene.
Upon his hond he bare for his deduit
An egle tame, as any lily whit.
An hundred lordes had he with him there,
All armed save hir hedes in all hir gere,
Ful richely in alle manere thinges.
For trusteth wel, that erles, dukes, kinges
Were gathered in this noble compagnie,
For love, and for encrese of chevalrie.
About this king ther ran on every part
Ful many a tame leon and leopart.

    And in this wise, these lordes all and some
Ben on the Sonday to the citee come
Abouten prime, and in the toun alight.

    This Theseus, this duk, this worthy knight,
Whan he had brought hem into his citee,

1   F

And inned hem, everich at his degree,
He festeth hem, and doth so gret labour
To esen hem, and don hem all honour,
That yet men wenen that no mannes wit
Of non estat ne coud amenden it.
The minstralcie, the service at the feste,
The grete yeftes to the most and leste,
The riche array of Theseus paleis,
Ne who sate first ne last upon the deis,
What ladies fayrest ben or best dancing,
Or which of hem can carole best or sing,
Ne who most felingly speketh of love;
What haukes sitten on the perche above,
What houndes liggen on the floor adoun,
Of all this now make I no mentioun;
But of the effect; that thinketh me the beste;
Now cometh the point, and herkeneth if you leste.

The Sonday night, or day began to spring,
Whan Palamon the larke herde sing,
Although it n'ere not day by houres two,
Yet sang the larke, and Palamon right tho
With holy herte, and with an high corage
He rose, to wenden on his pilgrimage
Unto the blisful Citherea benigne,
I mene Venus, honourable and digne.
And in hire houre, he walketh forth a pas
Unto the listes, ther hire temple was,
And doun he kneleth, and with humble chere
And herte sore, he sayde as ye shul here.

Fayrest of fayre, o lady min Venus,
Daughter to Jove, and spouse of Vulcanus,
Thou glader of the mount of Citheron,
For thilke love thou haddest to Adon
Have pitee on my bitter teres smert,

And take myn humble praier at thin herte.
   Alas! I ne have no langage to tell
The effecte, ne the torment of min hell;
Min herte may min harmes not bewrey;
I am so confuse, that I cannot say.
But mercy, lady bright, that knowest wele
My thought, and seest what harmes that I fele,
Consider all this, and rue upon my sore,
As wisly as I shall for evermore,
Emforth my might, thy trewe servant be,
And holden werre alway with chastite:
That make I min avow, so ye me helpe.
I kepe nought of armes for to yelpe,
Ne axe I nat to-morwe to have victorie,
Ne renoun in this cas, ne vaine glorie
Of pris of armes, blowen up and doun,
But I wold have fully possessioun
Of Emelie, and die in hire servise;
Find thou the manere how, and in what wise.
I rekke not, but it may better be,
To have victorie of hem, or they of me,
So that I have my lady in min armes.
For though so be that Mars is god of armes,
Your vertue is so grete in heven above,
That if you liste, I shal wel have my love.
Thy temple wol I worship evermo,
And on thin auter, wher I ride or go,
I wol don sacrifice, and fires bete.
And if ye wol not so, my lady swete,
Than pray I you, to-morwe with a spere
That Arcita me thurgh the herte bere.
Than rekke I not, whan I have lost my lif,
Though that Arcita win hire to his wif.
This is the effecte and ende of my praiere;

Yeve me my love, thou blisful lady dere.

Whan the orison was don of Palamon,
His sacrifice he did, and that anon,
Full pitously, with alle circumstances,
All tell I not as now his observances.
But at the last the statue of Venus shoke,
And made a signe, wherby that he toke,
That his praiere accepted was that day.
For though the signe shewed a delay,
Yet wist he wel that granted was his bone;
And with glad herte he went him home ful sone.

The thridde houre inequal that Palamon
Began to Venus temple for to gon,
Up rose the sonne, and up rose Emelie,
And to the temple of Diane gan hie.
Hire maydens, that she thider with hire ladde,
Ful redily with hem the fire they hadde,
Th'encense, the clothes, and the remenant all,
That to the sacrifice longen shall.
The hornes ful of mede, as was the gise,
Ther lakked nought to don hire sacrifise.
Smoking the temple, ful of clothes fayre,
This Emelie with herte debonaire
Hire body wesshe with water of a well.
But how she did hire rite I dare not tell;
But it be any thing in general;
And yet it were a game to heren all;
To him that meneth wel it n'ere no charge:
But it is good a man to ben at large.
Hire bright here kembed was, untressed all.
A coroune of a grene oke cerial
Upon hire hed was set ful fayre and mete.
Two fires on the auter gan she bete,
And did hire thinges, as men may behold

In Stace of Thebes, and these bokes old.

Whan kindled was the fire, with pitous chere
Unto Diane she spake, as ye may here.

O chaste goddesse of the wodes grene,
To whom both heven and erthe and see is sene,
Quene of the regne of Pluto, derke and lowe,
Goddesse of maydens, that min herte hast knowe
Ful many a yere, and wost what I desire,
As kepe me fro thy vengeance and thin ire,
That Atteon aboughte cruelly:
Chaste goddesse, wel wotest thou that I
Desire to ben a mayden all my lif,
Ne never wol I be no love ne wif.
I am (thou wost) yet of thy compagnie,
A mayde, and love hunting and venerie,
And for to walken in the wodes wilde,
And not to ben a wif, and be with childe.
Nought wol I knowen compagnie of man.
Now helpe me, lady, sith ye may and can,
For tho three formes that thou hast in thee.
And Palamon, that hath swiche love to me,
And eke Arcite, that loveth me so sore,
This grace I praie thee withouten more,
As sende love and pees betwix hem two:
And fro me torne away hir hertes so,
That all hir hote love, and hir desire,
And all hir besy torment, and hir fire
Be queinte, or torned in another place.
And if so be thou wolt not do me grace,
Or if my destinee be shapen so,
That I shall nedes have on of hem two,
As sende me him that most desireth me.

Behold, goddesse of clene chastite,
The bitter teres, that on my chekes fall.

Sin thou art mayde, and keper of us all,
My maydenhed thou kepe and wel conserve,
And while I live, a mayde I wol thee serve.

The fires brenne upon the auter clere,
While Emelie was thus in hire praiere :
But sodenly she saw a sighte queinte.
For right anon on of the fires queinte,
And quiked again, and after that anon
That other fire was queinte, and all agon :
And as it queinte, it made a whisteling,
As don these brondes wet in hir brenning.
And at the brondes ende outran anon
As it were blody dropes many on :
For which so sore agast was Emelie,
That she was wel neigh mad, and gan to crie,
For she ne wiste what it signified ;
But only for the fere thus she cried,
And wept, that it was pitee for to here.

And therwithall Diane gan appere
With bowe in hond, right as an hunteresse,
And sayde ; doughter, stint thin hevinesse.
Among the goddes highe it is affermed,
And by eterne word written and confermed,
Thou shalt be wedded unto on of tho,
That han for thee so mochel care and wo :
But unto which of hem I may not tell.
Farewel, for here I may no longer dwell.
The fires which that on min auter brenne,
Shal thee declaren er that thou go henne,
Thin aventure of love, as in this cas.

And with that word, the arwes in the cas
Of the goddesse clatteren fast and ring,
And forth she went, and made a vanishing,
For which this Emelie astonied was,

And sayde; what amounteth this, alas!
I putte me in thy protection,
Diane, and in thy disposition.
And home she goth anon the nexte way.
This is the effecte, ther n'is no more to say.

The nexte houre of Mars folwing this
Arcite unto the temple walked is
Of fierce Mars, to don his sacrifise
With all the rites of his payen wise.
With pitous herte and high devotion,
Right thus to Mars he sayde his orison.

O strange god, that in the regnes cold
Of Trace honoured art, and lord yhold,
And hast in every regne and every lond
Of armes all the bridel in thin hond,
And hem fortunest as thee list devise,
Accept of me my pitous sacrifise.
If so be that my youthe may deserve,
And that my might be worthy for to serve
Thy godhed, that I may ben on of thine,
Than praie I thee to rewe upon my pine,
For thilke peine, and thilke hote fire,
In which thou whilom brendest for desire
Whanne that thou usedest the beautee
Of fayre yonge Venus, freshe and free,
And haddest hire in armes at thy wille:
Although thee ones on a time misfille,
Whan Vulcanus had caught thee in his las,
And fond the ligging by his wif, alas!
For thilke sorwe that was tho in thin herte,
Have reuthe as wel upon my peines smerte.

I am yonge and unkonning, as thou wost,
And, as I trow, with love offended most,
That ever was ony lives creature:

For she, that doth me all this wo endure,
Ne recceth never, whether I sinke or flete.
And wel I wot, or she me mercy hete,
I moste with strengthe win hire in the place:
And wel I wot, withouten helpe or grace
Of thee, ne may my strengthe not availle :
Than helpe me, lord, to-morwe in my bataille,
For thilke fire that whilom brenned thee,
As wel as that this fire now brenneth me ;
And do, that I to-morwe may han victorie.
Min be the travaille, and thin be the glorie.
Thy soveraine temple wol I most honouren
Of ony place, and alway most labouren
In thy plesance and in thy craftes strong.
And in thy temple I wol my baner hong,
And all the armes of my compagnie,
And evermore, until that day I die,
Eterne fire I wol beforne thee finde,
And eke to this avow I wol me binde.
My berd, my here that hangeth long adoun,
That never yet felt non offension
Of rasour ne of shere, I wol thee yeve,
And ben thy trewe servant while I live.
Now, lord, have reuthe upon my sorwes sore,
Yeve me the victorie, I axe thee no more.

The praier stint of Arcita the stronge,
The ringes on the temple dore that honge,
And eke the dores clattereden ful faste,
Of which Arcita somwhat him agaste.
The fires brent upon the auter bright,
That it gan all the temple for to light;
A swete smell anon the ground up yaf,
And Arcita anon his hond up haf,
And more encense into the fire he cast,

With other rites mo, and at the last
The statue of Mars began his hauberke ring;
And with that soun he herd a murmuring
Ful low and dim, that sayde thus, Victorie.
For which he yaf to Mars honour and glorie.

And thus with joye, and hope wel to fare,
Arcite anon unto his inne is fare,
As fayn as foul is of the brighte sonne.

And right anon swiche strif ther is begonne
For thilke granting, in the heven above,
Betwixen Venus the goddesse of love,
And Mars the sterne god armipotent,
That Jupiter was besy it to stent:
Til that the pale Saturnus the colde,
That knew so many of aventures olde,
Fond in his olde experience and art,
That he ful sone hath plesed every part.
As sooth is sayd, elde hath gret avantage,
In elde is bothe wisdom and usage:
Men may the old out-renne, but not out-rede.

Saturne anon, to stenten strif and drede,
Al be it that it is again his kind,
Of all this strif he gan a remedy find.

My dere doughter Venus, quod Saturne,
My cours, that hath so wide for to turne,
Hath more power than wot any man.
Min is the drenching in the see so wan,
Min is the prison in the derke cote,
Min is the strangel and hanging by the throte,
The murmure, and the cherles rebelling,
The groyning, and the prive empoysoning.
I do vengeance and pleine correction,
While I dwell in the signe of the leon.
Min is the ruine of the highe halles,

The falling of the toures and of the walles
Upon the minour, or the carpenter:
I slew Sampson in shaking the piler.
Min ben also the maladies colde,
The derke tresons, and the castes olde:
My loking is the fader of pestilence.
Now wepe no more, I shal do diligence,
That Palamon, that is thin owen knight,
Shal have his lady, as thou hast him hight.
Thogh Mars shal help his knight yet natheles.
Betwixen you ther mot somtime be pees:
All be ye not of o complexion,
That causeth all day swiche division.
I am thin ayel, redy at thy will;
Wepe now no more, I shal thy lust fulfill.

Now wol I stenten of the goddes above,
Of Mars, and of Venus goddesse of love,
And tellen you as plainly as I can
The gret effect, for which that I began.

Gret was the feste in Athenes thilke day,
And eke the lusty seson of that May
Made every wight to ben in swiche plesance,
That all that monday justen they and dance,
And spenden it in Venus highe servise.
But by the cause that they shulden rise
Erly a-morwe for to seen the fight,
Unto hir reste wenten they at night.
And on the morwe whan the day gan spring,
Of hors and harneis noise and clattering
Ther was in the hostelries all aboute:
And to the paleis rode ther many a route
Of lordes, upon stedes and palfreis.

Ther mayst thou see devising of harneis
So uncouth and so riche, and wrought so wele

Of goldsmithry, of brouding, and of stele;
The sheldes brighte, testeres, and trappures;
Gold-hewen helmes, hauberkes, cote-armures;
Lordes in parementes on hir courseres,
Knightes of retenue, and eke squieres,
Nailing the speres, and helmes bokeling,
Gniding of sheldes, with lainers lacing;
Ther as nede is, they weren nothing idel:
The fomy stedes on the golden bridel
Gnawing, and fast the armureres also
With file and hammer priking to and fro;
Yemen on foot, and communes many on
With shorte staves, thicke as they may gon;
Pipes, trompes, nakeres, and clariounes,
That in the bataille blowen blody sounes;
The paleis ful of peple up and doun,
Here three, ther ten, holding hir questioun,
Devining of these Theban knightes two.
Som sayden thus, som sayde il shal be so;
Som helden with him with the blacke berd,
Som with the balled, som with the thick herd;
Som saide he loked grim, and wolde fighte:
He hath a sparth of twenty pound of wighte.
　　Thus was the halle full of devining
Long after that the sonne gan up spring.
The gret Theseus that of his slepe is waked
With minstralcie and noise that was maked,
Held yet the chambre of his paleis riche,
Til that the Theban knightes bothe yliche
Honoured were, and to the paleis fette.
　　Duk Theseus is at a window sette,
Araied right as he were a god in trone:
The peple preseth thiderward ful sone
Him for to seen, and don high reverence,

And eke to herken his heste and his sentence.

An heraud on a scaffold made an o,
Til that the noise of the peple was ydo:
And whan he saw the peple of noise al still,
Thus shewed he the mighty dukes will.

The lord hath of his high discretion
Considered, that it were destruction
To gentil blood, to fighten in the gise
Of mortal bataille now in this emprise:
Wherfore to shapen that they shul not die,
He wol his firste purpos modifie.

No man therfore, up peine of losse of lif,
No maner shot, ne pollax, ne short knif
Into the listes send, or thider bring.
Ne short swerd for to stike with point biting
No man ne draw, ne bere it by his side.
Ne no man shal unto his felaw ride
But o cours, with a sharpe ygrounden spere:
Foin if him list on foot, himself to were.
And he that is at meschief, shal be take,
And not slaine, but be brought unto the stake,
That shal ben ordeined on eyther side,
Thider he shal by force, and ther abide.
And if so fall, the chevetain be take
On eyther side, or elles sleth his make,
No longer shal the tourneying ylast.
God spede you; goth forth and lay on fast.
With longe swerd and with mase fighteth your fill.
Goth now your way; this is the lordes will.

The vois of the peple touched to the heven,
So loude crieden they with mery steven:
God save swiche a lord that is so good,
He wilneth no destruction of blood.

Up gon the trompes and the melodie,

And to the listes rit the compagnie
By ordinance, thurghout the cite large,
Hanged with cloth of gold, and not with sarge.
Ful like a lord this noble duk gan ride,
And these two Thebans upon eyther side :
And after rode the quene and Emelie,
And after that another compagnie
Of on and other, after hir degree.
And thus they passen thurghout the citee,
And to the listes comen they be time :
It n'as not of the day yet fully prime.

 Whan set was Theseus ful rich and hie,
Ipolita the quene, and Emelie,
And other ladies in degrees aboute,
Unto the setes preseth all the route.
And westward, thurgh the gates under Mart,
Arcite, and eke the hundred of his part,
With baner red, is entred right anon ;
And in the selve moment Palamon
Is, under Venus, estward in the place,
With baner white, and hardy chere and face.
In all the world, to seken up and doun,
So even without variatioun
Ther n'ere swiche compagnies never twey.
For ther was non so wise that coude sey,
That any hadde of other avantage
Of worthinesse, ne of estat, ne age,
So even were they chosen for to gesse.
And in two renges fayre they hem dresse.
Whan that hir names red were everich on,
That in hir nombre gile were ther non,
Tho were the gates shette, and cried was loude ;
Do now your devoir, yonge knightes proude.
 The heraudes left hir priking up and doun.

Now ringen trompes loud and clarioun.
Ther is no more to say, but est and west
In gon the speres sadly in the rest;
In goth the sharpe spore into the side.
Ther see men who can juste, and who can ride.
Ther shiveren shaftes upon sheldes thicke;
He feleth thurgh the herte-spone the pricke.
Up springen speres twenty foot on highte;
Out gon the swerdes as the silver brighte.
The helmes they to-hewen, and to-shrede;
Out brest the blod, with sterne stremes rede.
With mighty maces the bones they to-breste.
He thurgh the thickest of the throng gan threste.
Ther stomblen stedes strong, and doun goth all.
He rolleth under foot as doth a ball.
He foineth on his foo with a tronchoun,
And he him hurtleth with his hors adoun.
He thurgh the body is hurt, and sith ytake
Maugre his hed, and brought unto the stake,
As forword was, right ther he must abide.
Another lad is on that other side.
And somtime doth hem Theseus to rest,
Hem to refresh, and drinken if hem lest.

  Ful oft a day han thilke Thebanes two
Togeder met, and wrought eche other wo:
Unhorsed hath eche other of hem twey.
Ther n'as no tigre in the vale of Galaphey,
Whan that hire whelpe is stole, whan it is lite,
So cruel on the hunt, as is Arcite
For jalous herte upon this Palamon:
Ne in Belmarie ther n'is so fell leon,
That hunted is, or for his hunger wood,
Ne of his prey desireth so the blood,
As Palamon to sleen his foo Arcite.

The jalous strokes on hir helmes bite ;
Out renneth blood on both hir sides rede.

Somtime an ende ther is of every dede.
For er the sonne unto the reste went,
The stronge king Emetrius gan hent
This Palamon, as he fought with Arcite,
And made his swerd depe in his flesh to bite.
And by the force of twenty is he take
Unyolden, and ydrawen to the stake.
And in the rescous of this Palamon
The stronge king Licurge is borne adoun :
And king Emetrius for all his strengthe
Is borne out of his sadel a swerdes lengthe,
So hitte him Palamon or he were take :
But all for nought, he was brought to the stake :
His hardy herte might him helpen naught,
He moste abiden, whan that he was caught,
By force, and eke by composition.

Who sorweth now but woful Palamon ?
That moste no more gon again to fight.
And whan that Theseus had seen that sight,
Unto the folk that foughten thus eche on,
He cried, ho ! no more, for it is don.
I wol be trewe juge, and not partie.
Arcite of Thebes shal have Emelie,
That by his fortune hath hire fayre ywonne.

Anon ther is a noise of peple begonne
For joye of this, so loud and high withall,
It semed that the listes shulden fall.

What can now fayre Venus don above ?
What saith she now ? what doth this quene of
But wepeth so, for wanting of hire will, [love ?
Til that hire teres in the listes fill :
She sayde : I am ashamed, doutelees.

Saturnus sayde : Daughter, hold thy pees.
Mars hath his will, his knight hath all his bone,
And by min hed thou shalt ben esed sone.

The trompoures with the loude minstralcie,
The heraudes, that so loude yell and crie,
Ben in hir joye for wele of Dan Arcite.
But herkeneth me, and stenteth noise a lite,
Whiche a miracle ther befell anon.

This fierce Arcite hath of his helme ydon,
And on a courser for to shew his face
He priketh endelong the large place,
Loking upward upon this Emelie ;
And she again him cast a frendlich eye,
(For women, as to speken in commune,
They folwen all the favour of fortune)
And was all his in chere, as his in herte.
Out of the ground a fury infernal sterte,
From Pluto sent, at requeste of Saturne,
For which his hors for fere gan to turne,
And lepte aside, and foundred as he lepe :
And er that Arcite may take any kepe,
He pight him on the pomel of his hed,
That in the place he lay as he were ded,
His brest to-brosten with his sadel bow.
As blake he lay as any cole or crow,
So was the blood yronnen in his face.

Anon he was yborne out of the place
With herte sore, to Theseus paleis.
Tho was he corven out of his harneis,
And in a bed ybrought ful fayre and blive,
For he was yet in memorie and live,
And alway crying after Emelie.

Duk Theseus, with all his compagnie,
Is comen home to Athenes his citee,

With alle blisse and gret solempnite.
Al be it that this aventure was falle,
He n'olde not discomforten hem alle.
Men sayden eke, that Arcite shal not die,
He shal ben heled of his maladie.
And of another thing they were as fayn,
That of hem alle was ther non yslain,
Al were they sore yhurt, and namely on,
That with a spere was thirled his brest bone.
To other woundes, and to broken armes,
Som hadden salves, and som hadden charmes:
And fermacies of herbes, and eke save
They dronken, for they wold hir lives have.
For which this noble duk, as he wel can,
Comforteth and honoureth every man,
And made revel all the longe night,
Unto the strange lordes, as was right.
Ne ther n'as holden no discomforting,
But as at justes or a tourneying ;
For sothly ther n'as no discomfiture,
For falling n'is not but an aventure.
Ne to be lad by force unto a stake
Unyolden, and with twenty knightes take,
O person all alone, withouten mo,
And haried forth by armes, foot, and too,
And eke his stede driven forth with staves,
With footmen, bothe yemen and eke knaves,
It was aretted him no vilanie :
Ther may no man clepen it cowardie.
For which anon duk Theseus let crie,
To stenten alle rancour and envie,
The gree as wel of o side as of other,
And eyther side ylike, as others brother :
And yave hem giftes after hir degree,

I   G

And helde a feste fully dayes three :
And conveyed the kinges worthily
Out of his toun a journee largely.
And home went every man the righte way,
Ther n'as no more, but farewel, have good day.
Of this bataille I wol no more endite,
But speke of Palamon and of Arcite.

Swelleth the brest of Arcite, and the sore
Encreseth at his herte more and more.
The clotered blood, for any leche-craft,
Corrumpeth, and is in his bouke ylaft,
That neyther veine-blood, ne ventousing,
Ne drinke of herbes may ben his helping.
The vertue expulsif, or animal,
Fro thilke vertue cleped natural,
Ne may the venime voiden, ne expell.
The pipes of his longes gan to swell,
And every lacerte in his brest adoun
Is shent with venime and corruptioun.
Him gaineth neyther, for to get his lif,
Vomit upward, ne dounward laxatif;
All is to-brosten thilke region ;
Nature hath now no domination.
And certainly ther nature wol not werche,
Farewel physike ; go bere the man to cherche.
This is all and som, that Arcite moste die.
For which he sendeth after Emelie,
And Palamon, that was his cosin dere.
Than sayd he thus, as ye shuln after here.

Nought may the woful spirit in myn herte
Declare o point of all my sorwes smerte
To you, my lady, that I love most ;
But I bequethe the service of my gost
To you aboven every creäture,

Sin that my lif ne may no lenger dure.

Alas the wo ! alas the peines stronge,
That I for you have suffered, and so longe !
Alas the deth ! alas min Emelie !
Alas departing of our compagnie !
Alas min hertes quene ! alas my wif !
Min hertes ladie, ender of my lif !
What is this world ? what axen men to have ?
Now with his love, now in his colde grave
Alone withouten any compagnie.
Farewel my swete, farewel min Emelie,
And softe take me in your armes twey,
For love of God, and herkeneth what I sey.

I have here with my cosin Palamon
Had strif and rancour many a day agon
For love of you, and for my jalousie.
And Jupiter so wis my soule gie,
To speken of a servant proprely,
With alle circumstances trewely,
That is to sayn, trouth, honour, and knighthede,
Wisdom, humblesse, estat, and high kinrede,
Fredom, and all that longeth to that art,
So Jupiter have of my soule part,
As in this world right now ne know I non,
So worthy to be loved as Palamon,
That serveth you, and wol don all his lif.
And if that ever ye shal ben a wif,
Foryete not Palamon, the gentil man.

And with that word his speche faille began.
For from his feet up to his brest was come
The cold of deth, that had him overnome.
And yet moreover in his armes two
The vital strength is lost, and all ago.
Only the intellect, withouten more,

That dwelled in his herte sike and sore,
Gan faillen, whan the herte felte deth;
Dusked his eyen two, and failled his breth.
But on his ladie yet cast he his eye;
His laste word was; Mercy, Emelie!
His spirit changed hous, and wente ther,
As I came never I cannot tellen wher.
Therfore I stent, I am no divinistre;
Of soules find I not in this registre.
Ne me lust not th' opinions to telle   [dwelle.
Of hem, though that they writen wher they
Arcite is cold, ther Mars his soule gie.
Now wol I speken forth of Emelie.

    Shright Emelie, and houleth Palamon,
And Theseus his sister toke anon
Swouning, and bare hire from the corps away.
What helpeth it to tarien forth the day,
To tellen how she wep both even and morwe?
For in swiche cas wimmen have swiche sorwe,
Whan that hir housbonds ben fro hem ago,
That for the more part they sorwen so,
Or elles fallen in swiche maladie,
That atte laste certainly they die.

    Infinite ben the sorwes and the teres
Of olde folk, and folk of tendre yeres,
In all the toun fer deth of this Theban:
For him ther wepeth bothe childe and man.
So gret a weping was ther non certain,
Whan Hector was ybrought, all fresh yslain
To Troy, alas! the pitee that was there,
Cratching of chekes, rending eke of here.
Why woldest thou be ded? thise women crie,
And haddest gold ynough, and Emelie.

    No man might gladen this duk Theseus,

Saving his olde fader Egeus,
That knew this worldes transmutatioun,
As he had seen it chaungen up and doun,
Joye after wo, and wo after gladnesse ;
And shewed him ensample and likenesse.

Right as ther died never man (quod he)
That he ne lived in erthe in som degree,
Right so ther lived never man (he seyd)
In all this world, that somtime he ne deyd.
This world n'is but a thurghfare ful of wo,
And we ben pilgrimes, passing to and fro :
Deth is an end of every worldes sore.

And over all this yet said he mochel more
To this effect, ful wisely to enhort
The peple, that they shuld hem recomfort.

Duk Theseus with all his besy cure
He casteth now, wher that the sepulture
Of good Arcite may best ymaked be,
And eke most honourable in his degree.
And at the last he toke conclusion,
That ther as first Arcite and Palamon
Hadden for love the bataille hem betwene,
That in that selve grove, sote and grene,
Ther as he hadde his amorous desires,
His complaint, and for love his hote fires,
He wolde make a fire, in which the office
Of funeral he might all accomplise ;
And lete anon commande to hack and hewe
The okes old, and lay hem on a rew
In culpons, wel araied for to brenne.
His officers with swifte feet they renne
And ride anon at his commandement.
And after this, this Theseus hath sent
After a bere, and it all overspradde

With cloth of gold, the richest that he hadde;
And of the same suit he cladde Arcite.
Upon his hondes were his gloves white,
Eke on his hed a croune of laurer grene,
And in his hond a swerd ful bright and kene.
He laid him bare the visage on the bere,
Therwith he wept that pitee was to here.
And for the peple shulde seen him alle,
Whan it was day he brought him to the halle,
That roreth of the crying and the soun.

Tho came this woful Theban Palamon
With flotery berd, and ruggy asshy heres,
In clothes blake, ydropped all with teres,
And (passing over of weping Emelie)
The reufullest of all the compagnie.

And in as much as the service shuld be
The more noble and riche in his degree,
Duk Theseus let forth three stedes bring,
That trapped were in stele all glittering,
And covered with the armes of Dan Arcite.
And eke upon these stedes gret and white
Ther saten folk, of which on bare his sheld,
Another his spere up in his hondes held;
The thridde bare with him his bow Turkeis,
Of brent gold was the cas and the harneis:
And riden forth a pas with sorweful chere
Toward the grove, as ye shul after here.

The noblest of the Grekes that ther were
Upon hir shuldres carrieden the bere,
With slacke pas, and eyen red and wete,
Thurghout the citee, by the maister strete,
That sprad was all with black, and wonder hie
Right of the same is all the strete ywrie.
Upon the right hand went olde Egeus,

And on that other side duk Theseus,
With vessels in hir hond of gold ful fine,
All ful of hony, milk, and blood, and wine;
Eke Palamon, with ful gret compagnie:
And after that came woful Emelie,
With fire in hond, as was that time the gise,
To don the office of funeral service.

High labour, and ful gret apparailling
Was at the service of that fire making,
That with his grene top the heven raught,
And twenty fadom of brede the armes straught:
This is to sain, the boughes were so brode.
Of stre first ther was laied many a lode.

But how the fire was maked up on highte,
And eke the names how the trees highte,
As oke, fir, birch, aspe, alder, holm, poplere,
Wilow, elm, plane, ash, box, chestein, lind, lau-
Maple, thorn, beche, hasel, ew, whipultre, [rere,
How they were feld, shal not be told for me; [rere,
Ne how the goddes rannen up and doun
Disherited of hir habitatioun,
In which they woneden in rest and pees,
Nimphes, Faunes, and Amadriades;
Ne how the bestes, and the briddes alle
Fledden for fere, whan the wood gan falle;
Ne how the ground agast was of the light,
That was not wont to see the sonne bright;
Ne how the fire was couched first with stre,
And than with drie stickes cloven a-thre,
And than with grene wood and spicerie,
And than with cloth of gold and with perrie,
And gerlonds hanging with ful many a flour,
The mirre, th'encense also with swete odour;
Ne how Arcita lay among all this,

Ne what richesse about his body is ;
Ne how that Emelie, as was the gise,
Put in the fire of funeral service ;
Ne how she swouned whan she made the fire,
Ne what she spake, ne what was hir desire ;
Ne what jewelles men in the fire caste,
Whan that the fire was gret and brente faste ;
Ne how som cast hir sheld, and som hir spere,
And of hir vestimentes, which they were,
And cuppes full of wine, and milk, and blood,
Into the fire, that brent as it were wood ;
Ne how the Grekes with a huge route
Three times riden all the fire aboute
Upon the left hond, with a loud shouting,
And thries with hir speres clatering ;
And thries how the ladies gan to crie ;
Ne how that led was homeward Emelie ;
Ne how Arcite is brent to ashen cold ;
Ne how the liche-wake was yhold
All thilke night, ne how the Grekes play.
The wake-plaies ne kepe I not to say :
Who wrestled best naked, with oile enoint,
Ne who that bare him best in no disjoint.
I woll not tellen eke how they all gon
Home til Athenes whan the play is don ;
But shortly to the point now wol I wende,
And maken of my longe tale an ende.

By processe and by lengthe of certain yeres
All stenten is the mourning and the teres
Of Grekes, by on general assent.
Than semeth me ther was a parlement
At Athenes, upon certain points and cas :
Amonges the which points yspoken was
To have with certain contrees alliance

And have of Thebanes fully obeisance.
For which this noble Theseus anon
Let senden after gentil Palamon,
Unwist of him, what was the cause and why :
But in his blacke clothes sorwefully
He came at his commandement on hie ;
Tho sente Theseus for Emelie.

Whan they were set, and husht was al the place,
And Theseus abiden hath a space,
Or any word came from his wise brest
His eyen set he ther as was his lest,
And with a sad visage he siked still,
And after that right thus he sayd his will.

The firste mover of the cause above
Whan he firste made the fayre chaine of love,
Gret was th'effect, and high was his entent ;
Wel wist he why, and what therof he ment :
For with that fayre chaine of love he bond
The fire, the air, the watre, and the lond
In certain bondes, that they may not flee :
That same prince and mover eke (quod he)
Hath stablisht, in this wretched world adoun,
Certain of dayes and duration
To all that are engendred in this place,
Over the which day they ne mow not pace,
Al mow they yet dayes wel abrege.
Ther nedeth non autoritee allege,
For it is preved by experience,
But that me lust declaren my sentence.
Than may men by this ordre wel discerne,
That thilke mover stable is and eterne.
Wel may men knowen, but it be a fool,
That every part deriveth from his hool.
For nature hath not taken his beginning

Of no partie ne cantel of a thing,
But of a thing that parfit is and stable,
Descending so, til it be corrumpable.
And therfore of his wise purveyance
He hath so wel beset his ordinance,
That speces of thinges and progressions
Shullen enduren by successions,
And not eterne, withouten any lie:
This maiest thou understand and seen at eye.
Lo th' oke, that hath so long a norishing
Fro the time that it ginneth first to spring,
And hath so long a lif, as ye may see,
Yet at the laste wasted is the tree.
Considereth eke, how that the harde stone
Under our feet, on which we trede and gon,
It wasteth, as it lieth by the wey.
The brode river somtime wexeth drey.
The grete tounes see we wane and wende.
Than may ye see that all thing hath an ende.
Of man and woman see we wel also,
That nedes in on of the termes two,
That is to sayn, in youthe or elles age,
He mote be ded, the king as shall a page;
Som in his bed, som in the depe see,
Som in the large feld, as ye may see:
Ther helpeth nought, all goth that ilke wey:
Than may I sayn that alle thing mote dey.
What maketh this but Jupiter the king?
The which is prince, and cause of alle thing,
Converting alle unto his propre wille,
From which it is derived, soth to telle.
And here-againes no creature on live
Of no degree availleth for to strive.
Than is it wisdom, as it thinketh me,

To maken vertue of necessite,
And take it wel, that we may not eschewe,
And namely that to us all is dewe.
And who so grutcheth ought, he doth folie,
And rebel is to him that all may gie.
And certainly a man hath most honour
To dien in his excellence and flour,
Whan he is siker of his goode name.
Than hath he don his frend, ne him, no shame;
And glader ought his frend ben of his deth,
Whan with honour is yolden up his breth,
Than whan his name appalled is for age;
For all foryetten is his vassallage.
Than is it best, as for a worthy fame,
To dien whan a man is best of name.
The contrary of all this is wilfulnesse.
Why grutchen we? why have we hevinesse,
That good Arcite, of chivalry the flour,
Departed is, with dutee and honour,
Out of this foule prison of this lif?
Why grutchen here his cosin and his wif
Of his welfare, that loven him so wel?
Can he hem thank? nay, God wot, never a del,
That both his soule, and eke hemself offend,
And yet they mow hir lustes not amend.
    What may I conclude of this longe serie,
But after sorwe I rede us to be merie,
And thanken Jupiter of all his grace.
And er that we departen from this place,
I rede that we make of sorwes two
O parfit joye lasting evermo:
And loketh now wher most sorwe is herein,
Ther wol I firste amenden and begin.
    Sister, (quod he) this is my full assent,

With all th'avis here of my parlement,
That gentil Palamon, your owen knight,
That serveth you with will, and herte, and might,
And ever hath don, sin ye first him knew,
That ye shall of your grace upon him rew,
And taken him for husbond and for lord :
Lene me your hand, for this is oure accord.

Let see now of your womanly pitee.
He is a kinges brothers sone pardee,
And though he were a poure bachelere,
Sin he hath served you so many a yere,
And had for you so gret adversite,
It moste ben considered, leveth me.
For gentil mercy oweth to passen right.

Than sayd he thus to Palamon the knight ;
I trow ther nedeth litel sermoning
To maken you assenten to this thing.
Cometh ner, and take your lady by the hond.

Betwixen hem was maked anon the bond,
That highte matrimoine or mariage,
By all the conseil of the baronage.
And thus with alle blisse and melodie
Hath Palamon ywedded Emelie.
And God that all this wide world hath wrought,
Send him his love, that hath it dere ybought.
For now is Palamon in alle wele,
Living in blisse, in richesse, and in hele,
And Emelie him loveth so tendrely,
And he hire serveth al so gentilly,
That never was ther no word hem betwene
Of jalousie, ne of non other tene.

Thus endeth Palamon and Emelie ;
And God save all this fayre compagnie.

The Milleres Prologue.

WHAN that the Knight had thus his tale
  told,
In all the compagnie n'as ther yong ne old,
That he ne said it was a noble storie,
And worthy to be drawen to memorie;
And namely the gentiles everich on.
Our Hoste lough and swore, So mote I gon,
This goth aright; unbokeled is the male;
Let see now who shal tell another tale:
For trewely this game is wel begonne.
Now telleth ye, sire Monk, if that ye conne,
Somwhat, to quiten with the knightes tale.

  The Miller that for-dronken was all pale,
So that unethes upon his hors he sat,
He n'old avalen neither hood ne hat,
Ne abiden no man for his curtesie,
But in Pilates vois he gan to crie,
And swore by armes, and by blood, and bones,
I can a noble tale for the nones,
With which I wol now quite the knightes tale.

  Our Hoste saw that he was dronken of ale,
And sayd; abide, Robin, my leve brother,
Som better man shall tell us first another:
Abide, and let us werken thriftily.

  By Goddes soule (quod he) that wol not I,
For I wol speke, or elles go my way.

  Our Hoste answerd; Tell on a devil way;
Thou art a fool; thy wit is overcome.

Now herkeneth, quod the Miller, all and some :
But first I make a protestatioun,
That I am dronke, I know it by my soun :
And therfore if that I misspeke or say,
Wite it the ale of Southwerk, I you pray :
For I wol tell a legend and a lif
Both of a carpenter and of his wif,
How that a clerk hath set the wrightes cappe.

The Reve answerd and saide, Stint thy clappe.
Let be thy lewed dronken harlotrie.
It is a sinne, and eke a gret folie
To apeiren any man, or him defame,
And eke to bringen wives in swiche a name.
Thou mayst ynough of other thinges sain.

This dronken Miller spake ful sone again,
And sayde ; Leve brother Osewold,
Who hath no wif, he is no cokewold.
But I say not therfore that thou art on ;
Ther ben ful goode wives many on.
Why art thou angry with my tale now ?
I have a wif parde as wel as thou,
Yet n'olde I, for the oxen in my plough,
Taken upon me more than ynough
As demen of myself that I am on ;
I wol beleven wel that I am non.
An husbond shuld not ben inquisitif
Of Goddes privite, ne of his wif.
So he may finden Goddes foison there,
Of the remenant nedeth not to enquere.

What shuld I more say, but this Millere
He n'olde his wordes for no man forbere,
But told his cherles tale in his manere,
Me thinketh, that I shal reherse it here.
And therfore every gentil wight I pray,

For Goddes love as deme not that I say
Of evil entent, but that I mote reherse
Hir tales alle, al be they better or werse,
Or elles falsen som of my matere.
And therfore who so list it not to here,
Turne over the leef, and chese another tale,
For he shal find ynow bothe gret and smale,
Of storial thing that toucheth gentillesse,
And eke moralite, and holinesse.
Blameth not me, if that ye chese amis.
The Miller is a cherl, ye know wel this,
So was the Reve, (and many other mo)
And harlotrie they tolden bothe two.
Aviseth you now, and put me out of blame ;
And eke men shuld not make ernest of game.

The Milleres Tale.

WHILOM ther was dwelling in Oxenforde
A riche gnof, that gestes helde to borde,
And of his craft he was a carpenter.
With him ther was dwelling a poure scoler,
Had lerned art, but all his fantasie
Was turned for to lerne astrologie,
And coude a certain of conclusions
To demen by interrogations,
If that men asked him in certain houres,
Whan that men shulde have drought or elles
Or if men asked him what shulde falle [shoures :
Of every thing, I may not reken alle.
  This clerk was cleped hendy Nicholas ;

Of derne love he coude and of solas ;
And therto he was slie and ful prive,
And like a maiden meke for to se.
A chambre had he in that hostelrie
Alone, withouten any compagnie,
Ful fetisly ydight with herbes sote,
And he himself was swete as is the rote
Of licoris, or any setewale.
His almageste, and bokes gret and smale,
His astrelabre, longing for his art,
His augrim stones, layen faire apart
On shelves couched at his beddes hed,
His presse ycovered with a falding red.
And all above ther lay a gay sautrie,
On which he made on nightes melodie,
So swetely, that all the chambre rong :
And *Angelus ad virginem* he song.
And after that he song the kinges note ;
Ful often blessed was his mery throte.
And thus this swete clerk his time spent
After his frendes finding and his rent.

This carpenter had wedded new a wif,
Which that he loved more than his lif :
Of eightene yere she was I gesse of age.
Jalous he was, and held hire narwe in cage,
For she was wild and yonge, and he was old,
And demed himself belike a cokewold.
He knew not Caton, for his wit was rude,
That bade a man shulde wedde his similitude.
Men shulden wedden after hir estate,
For youthe and elde is often at debate.
But sithen he was fallen in the snare,
He most endure (as other folk) his care.

Fayre was this yonge wif, and therwithal

As any wesel hire body gent and smal.
A seint she wered, barred all of silk,
A barme-cloth eke as white as morwe milk
Upon hire lendes, ful of many a gore.
White was hire smok, and brouded all before
And eke behind on hire colere aboute
Of cole-black silk, within and eke withoute.
The tapes of hire white volupere
Were of the same suit of hire colere;
Hire fillet brode of silk, and set full hye:
And sikerly she had a likerous eye.
Ful smal ypulled were hire browes two,
And they were bent, and black as any slo.
She was wel more blisful on to see
Than is the newe perjenete tree;
And softer than the wolle is of a wether.

And by hire girdel heng a purse of lether,
Tasseled with silk, and perled with latoun.
In all this world to seken up and doun
Ther n'is no man so wise, that coude thenche
So gay a popelot, or swiche a wenche.
Ful brighter was the shining of hire hewe,
Than in the tour the noble yforged newe.
But of hire song, it was as loud and yerne,
As any swalow sitting on a berne.
Therto she coude skip, and make a game,
As any kid or calf folowing his dame.
Hire mouth was swete as braket or the meth,
Or hord of apples, laid in hay or heth.
Winsing she was, as is a joly colt,
Long as a mast, and upright as a bolt.
A broche she bare upon hire low colere,
As brode as is the bosse of a bokelere.
Hire shoon were laced on hire legges hie;

I   H

She was a primerole, a piggesnie,
For any lord to liggen in his bedde,
Or yet for any good yeman to wedde.

    Now sire, and eft sire, so befell the cas,
That on a day this hendy Nicholas
Fel with this yonge wif to rage and pleye,
While that hire husbond was at Oseney,
As clerkes ben ful subtil and ful queint.
And prively he caught hire by the queint,
And sayde ; Ywis, but if I have my will,
For derne love of thee, lemman, I spill.
And helde hire faste by the hanche bones,
And sayde ; Lemman, love me wel at ones,
Or I wol dien, al so God me save.

    And she sprong as a colt doth in the trave :
And with hire hed she writhed faste away,
And sayde ; I wol not kisse thee by my fay.
Why let be, (quod she) let be, Nicholas,
Or I wol crie out harow and alas.
Do way your hondes for your curtesie.

    This Nicholas gan mercy for to crie,
And spake so faire, and profered him so fast,
That she hire love him granted at the last,
And swore hire oth by Seint Thomas of Kent,
That she wold ben at his commandement,
Whan that she may hire leiser wel espie.
Myn husbond is so ful of jalousie,
That but ye waiten wel, and be prive,
I wot right wel I n'am but ded, quod she.
Ye mosten be ful derne as in this cas.

    Nay, therof care you not, quod Nicholas :
A clerk had litherly beset his while,
But if he coude a carpenter begile.
And thus they were accorded and ysworne

To waite a time, as I have said beforne.
Whan Nicholas had don thus every del,
And thacked hire about the lendes wel,
He kissed hire swete, and taketh his sautrie,
And plaieth fast, and maketh melodie.

Than fell it thus, that to the parish cherche
(Of Cristes owen werkes for to werche)
This good wif went upon a holy day:
Hire forehed shone as bright as any day,
So was it washen, whan she lete hire werk.

Now was ther of that chirche a parish clerk,
The which that was ycleped Absolon.
Crulle was his here, and as the gold it shon,
And strouted as a fanne large and brode;
Ful streight and even lay his joly shode.
His rode was red, his eyen grey as goos,
With Poules windowes corven on his shoos.
In hosen red he went ful fetisly.
Yclad he was ful smal and proprely,
All in a kirtel of a light waget;
Ful faire and thicke ben the pointes set.
And therupon he had a gay surplise,
As white as is the blosme upon the rise.

A mery child he was, so God me save;
Wel coud he leten blod, and clippe, and shave,
And make a chartre of lond, and a quitance.
In twenty manere coud he trip and dance,
(After the scole of Oxenforde tho)
And with his legges casten to and fro;
And playen songes on a smal ribible;
Therto he song somtime a loud quinible.
And as wel coud he play on a giterne.
In all the toun n'as brewhous ne taverne,
That he ne visited with his solas,

Ther as that any gaillard tapstere was.
But soth to say he was somdel squaimous
Of farting, and of speche dangerous.

This Absolon, that joly was and gay,
Goth with a censer on the holy day,
Censing the wives of the parish faste;
And many a lovely loke he on hem caste,
And namely on this carpenteres wif:
To loke on hire him thought a mery lif.
She was so propre, and swete, and likerous.
I dare wel sain, if she had ben a mous,
And he a cat, he wolde hire hente anon.

This parish clerk, this joly Absolon,
Hath in his herte swiche a love-longing,
That of no wif toke he non offering:
For curtesie, he sayd, he n'olde non.

The moone at night ful clere and brighte shon,
And Absolon his giterne hath ytake,
For paramours he thoughte for to wake.
And forth he goth, jolif and amorous,
Til he came to the carpenteres hous,
A litel after the cockes had ycrow,
And dressed him up by a shot window,
That was upon the carpenteres wal.
He singeth in his vois gentil and smal;
Now, dere lady,—if thy wille be,
I pray you that ye—wol rewe on me;
Ful wel accordant to his giterning.

This carpenter awoke, and herd him sing,
And spake unto his wif, and said anon,
What, Alison, heres thou not Absolon,
That chanteth thus under our boures wal?
And she answerd hire husbond therwithal;
Yes, God wot, John, I here him every del.

This passeth forth ; what wol ye bet than wel ?
Fro day to day this joly Absolon
So loveth hire, that him is wo-begon.
He waketh all the night, and all the day,
He kembeth his lockes brode, and made him gay.
He woeth hire by menes and brocage,
And swore he wolde ben hire owen page.
He singeth brokking as a nightingale.
He sent hire pinnes, methe, and spiced ale,
And wafres piping hot out of the glede :
And for she was of toun, he profered mede.
For som folk wol be wonnen for richesse,
And som for strokes, and som with gentillesse.

Somtime to shew his lightnesse and maistrie
He plaieth Herode on a skaffold hie.
But what availeth him as in this cas ?
So loveth she this hendy Nicholas,
That Absolon may blow the buckes horne :
He ne had for his labour but a scorne.
And thus she maketh Absolon hire ape,
And all his ernest tourneth to a jape.
Ful soth is this proverbe, it is no lie ;
Men say right thus alway ; the neighe slie
Maketh oft time the fer leef to be lothe.
For though that Absolon be wood or wrothe
Because that he fer was from hire sight,
This neighe Nicholas stood in his light.

Now bere thee wel, thou hendy Nicholas,
For Absolon may waile and sing alas.

And so befell that on a Saturday,
This carpenter was gon to Osenay,
And hendy Nicholas and Alison
Accorded ben to this conclusion,
That Nicholas shal shapen him a wile

This sely jalous husbond to begile;
And if so were the game went aright,
She shuld slepe in his armes alle night,
For this was hire desire and his also.
And right anon, withouten wordes mo,
This Nicholas no lenger wolde tarie,
But doth ful soft unto his chambre carie
Both mete and drinke for a day or twey.

And to hire husbond bad hire for to sey,
If that he axed after Nicholas,
She shulde say, she n'iste not wher he was;
Of all the day she saw him not with eye.
She trowed he was in som maladie,
For for no crie hire maiden coud him calle
He n'olde answer, for nothing that might falle.

Thus passeth forth all thilke Saturday,
That Nicholas still in his chambre lay,
And ete, and slept, and dide what him list
Til Sonday, that the sonne goth to rest.

This sely carpenter hath gret mervaile
Of Nicholas, or what thing might him aile,
And said; I am adrad by Seint Thomas
It stondeth not aright with Nicholas:
God shilde that he died sodenly.
This world is now ful tikel sikerly.
I saw to-day a corps yborne to cherche,
That now on Monday last I saw him werche.

Go up (quod he unto his knave) anon:
Clepe at his dore, or knocke with a ston:
Loke how it is, and tell me boldely.

This knave goth him up ful sturdely,
And at the chambre dore while that he stood,
He cried and knocked as that he were wood:
What how? what do ye, maister Nicholay?

How may ye slepen all the longe day?
But all for nought, he herde not a word.
An hole he fond ful low upon the bord,
Ther as the cat was wont in for to crepe,
And at that hole he loked in ful depe,
And at the last he had of him a sight.

This Nicholas sat ever gaping upright,
As he had kyked on the newe mone.

Adoun he goth, and telleth his maister sone,
In what array he saw this ilke man.

This carpenter to blissen him began,
And said; Now helpe us Seinte Frideswide.
A man wote litel what shal him betide.
This man is fallen with his astronomie
In som woodnesse or in som agonie.
I thought ay wel how that it shulde be.
Men shulde not knowe of Goddes privetee.
Ya blessed be alway a lewed man,
That nought but only his beleve can.
So ferd another clerk with astronomie;
He walked in the feldes for to prie
Upon the sterres, what ther shuld befalle,
Til he was in a marlepit yfalle.
He saw not that. But yet by Seint Thomas
Me reweth sore of hendy Nicholas:
He shal be rated of his studying,
If that I may, by Jesus heven king.

Get me a staf, that I may underspore
While that thou, Robin, hevest of the dore:
He shal out of his studying, as I gesse.
And to the chambre dore he gan him dresse.
His knave was a strong carl for the nones,
And by the haspe he haf it of at ones;
Into the flore the dore fell anon.

This Nicholas sat ay as stille as ston,
And ever he gaped upward into the eire.

This carpenter wend he were in despeire,
And hent him by the shulders mightily,
And shoke him hard, and cried spitously;
What, Nicholas? what how man? loke adoun:
Awake, and thinke on Cristes passioun.
I crouche thee from elves, and from wightes.
Therwith the nightspel said he anon rightes,
On foure halves of the hous aboute,
And on the threswold of the dore withoute.
Jesu Crist, and Seint Benedight,
Blisse this hous from every wicked wight,
Fro the nightes mare, the wite Pater-noster;
Wher wonest thou Seint Peters suster?

And at the last this hendy Nicholas
Gan for to siken sore, and said; Alas!
Shal all the world be lost eftsones now?

This carpenter answered; What saiest thou?
What? thinke on God, as we do, men that swinke.

This Nicholas answered; Fetch me a drinke;
And after wol I speke in privetee
Of certain thing that toucheth thee and me:
I wol tell it non other man certain.

This carpenter goth doun, and cometh again,
And brought of mighty ale a large quart;
And whan that eche of hem had dronken his part,
This Nicholas his dore faste shette,
And doun the carpenter by him he sette,
And saide; John, min hoste lefe and dere,
Thou shalt upon thy trouthe swere me here,
That to no wight thou shalt my conseil wrey:
For it is Cristes conseil that I say,
And if thou tell it man, thou art forlore:

For this vengeance thou shalt have therfore,
That if thou wreye me, thou shalt be wood.

Nay, Crist forbede it for his holy blood,
Quod tho this sely man; I am no labbe,
Ne though I say it, I n'am not lefe to gabbe.
Say what thou wolt, I shal it never telle
To child ne wif, by him that harwed helle.

Now, John, (quod Nicholas) I wol not lie,
I have yfounde in min astrologie,
As I have loked in the moone bright,
That now on Monday next, at quarter night,
Shal fall a rain, and that so wild and wood
That half so gret was never Noes flood.
This world (he said) in lesse than in an houre
Shal al be dreint, so hidous is the shoure:
Thus shal mankinde drenche, and lese hir lif

This carpenter answerd; Alas my wif!
And shal she drenche? alas min Alisoun!
For sorwe of this he fell almost adoun,
And said; Is ther no remedy in this cas?

Why yes, for God, quod hendy Nicholas;
If thou wolt werken after lore and rede;
Thou maist not werken after thin owen hede.
For thus saith Salomon, that was ful trewe;
Werke all by conseil, and thou shalt not rewe.
And if thou werken wolt by good conseil,
I undertake, withouten mast or seyl,
Yet shal I saven hire, and thee and me.
Hast thou not herd how saved was Noe,
Whan that our Lord had warned him beforne,
That al the world with water shuld be lorne?

Yes, (quod this carpenter) ful yore ago.

Hast thou not herd (quod Nicholas) also
The sorwe of Noe with his felawship,

Or that he mighte get his wif to ship?
Him had be lever, I dare wel undertake,
At thilke time, than all his wethers blake,
That she had had a ship hireself alone.
And therfore wost thou what is best to done?
This axeth hast, and of an hastif thing
Men may not preche and maken tarying.
Anon go get us fast into this in
A kneding trough or elles a kemelyn,
For eche of us; but loke that they ben large,
In which we mowen swimme as in a barge:
And have therin vitaille suffisant
But for a day; fie on the remenant;
The water shall aslake and gon away
Abouten prime upon the nexte day.
But Robin may not wete of this, thy knave,
Ne eke thy mayden Gille I may not save:
Axe not why: for though thou axe me,
I wol not tellen Goddes privetee.
Sufficeth thee, but if thy wittes madde,
To have as gret a grace as Noe hadde.
Thy wif shal I wel saven out of doute.
Go now thy way, and spede thee hereaboute.

But whan thou hast for hire, and thee, and me,
Ygeten us these kneding tubbes thre,
Than shalt thou hang hem in the roofe ful hie,
That no man of our purveyance espie:
And whan thou hast don thus as I have said,
And hast our vitaille faire in hem ylaid,
And eke an axe to smite the cord a-two
Whan that the water cometh, that we may go,
And breke an hole on high upon the gable
Unto the gardin ward, over the stable,
That we may frely passen forth our way,

Whan that the grete shoure is gon away.
Than shal thou swim as mery, I undertake,
As doth the white doke after hire drake:
Than wol I clepe, How Alison, how John,
Be mery: for the flood wol passe anon.
And thou wolt sain, Haile maister Nicholay,
Good morwe, I see thee wel, for it is day.
And than shall we be lordes all our lif
Of all the world, as Noe and his wif.
But of o thing I warne thee ful right,
Be wel avised on that ilke night,
That we ben entred into shippes bord,
That non of us ne speke not o word,
Ne clepe ne crie, but be in his praiere,
For it is Goddes owen heste dere.

Thy wif and thou moste hangen fer a-twinne,
For that betwixen you shal be no sinne,
No more in loking than ther shal in dede.
This ordinance is said; go, God thee spede.
To-morwe at night, whan men ben all aslepe,
Into our kneding tubbes wol we crepe,
And sitten ther, abiding Goddes grace.
Go now thy way, I have no lenger space
To make of this no lenger sermoning:
Men sain thus: send the wise, and say nothing:
Thou art so wise, it nedeth thee nought teche.
Go, save our lives, and that I thee beseche.

This sely carpenter goth forth his way,
Ful oft he said alas, and wala wa,
And to his wif he told his privetee,
And she was ware, and knew it bet than he
What all this queinte cast was for to sey.
But natheles she ferde as she wold dey,
And said; Alas! go forth thy way anon.

Helpe us to scape, or we be ded eche on.
I am thy trewe veray wedded wif;
Go, dere spouse, and helpe to save our lif.

Lo, what a gret thing is affection,
Men may die of imagination,
So depe may impression be take.
This sely carpenter beginneth quake:
Him thinketh veraily that he may see
Noes flood comen walwing as the see
To drenchen Alison, his hony dere.
He wepeth, waileth, maketh sory chere;
He siketh, with ful many a sory swough.
He goth, and geteth him a kneding trough,
And after a tubbe, and a kemelin,
And prively he sent hem to his in:
And heng hem in the roof in privetee.
His owen hond than made he ladders three,
To climben by the renges and the stalkes
Unto the tubbes honging in the balkes;
And vitailled bothe kemelin, trough and tubbe,
With bred and chese, and good ale in a jubbe,
Sufficing right ynow as for a day.

But er that he had made all this array,
He sent his knave, and eke his wenche also
Upon his nede to London for to go.
And on the Monday, whan it drew to night,
He shette his dore, withouten candel light,
And dressed all thing as it shulde bee.
And shortly up they clomben alle three.
They sitten stille wel a furlong way.
Now, *Pater noster*, clum, said Nicholay,
And clum, quod John, and clum, said Alison:
This carpenter said his devotion,
And still he sit, and biddeth his praiere,

Awaiting on the rain, if he it here.

The dede slepe, for wery besinesse,
Fell on this carpenter, right as I gesse,
Abouten curfew-time, or litel more.
For travaille of his gost he groneth sore,
And eft he routeth, for his hed mislay.
Doun of the ladder stalketh Nicholay,
And Alison ful soft adoun hire spedde.
Withouten wordes mo they went to bedde,
Ther as the carpenter was wont to lie ;
Ther was the revel, and the melodie.
And thus lith Alison, and Nicholas,
In besinesse of mirthe and in solas,
Til that the bell of *laudes* gan to ring,
And freres in the chancel gon to sing.

This parish clerk, this amorous Absolon,
That is for love alway so wo-begon,
Upon the Monday was at Osenay
With compagnie, him to disport and play ;
And asked upon cas a cloisterer
Ful prively after John the carpenter ;
And he drew him apart out of the chirche.
He said, I n'ot ; I saw him not here wirche
Sith Saturday ; I trow that he be went
For timbre, ther our abbot hath him sent.
For he is wont for timbre for to go,
And dwellen at the Grange a day or two :
Or elles he is at his hous certain.
Wher that he be, I cannot sothly sain.

This Absolon ful joly was and light,
And thoughte, now is time to wake al night,
For sikerly, I saw him nat stiring
About his dore, sin day began to spring.
So mote I thrive, I shal at cockes crow

Ful prively go knocke at his window,
That stant ful low upon his boures wall :
To Alison wol I now tellen all
My love-longing ; for yet I shall not misse,
That at the leste way I shal hire kisse.
Some maner comfort shal I have parfay,
My mouth hath itched all this longe day :
That is a signe of kissing at the leste.
All night me mette eke, I was at a feste.
Therfore I wol go slepe an houre or twey,
And all the night than wol I wake and pley.

Whan that the firste cock hath crowe, anon
Up rist this joly lover Absolon,
And him arayeth gay, at point devise.
But first he cheweth grein and licorise,
To smellen sote, or he had spoke with here.
Under his tonge a trewe love he bere,
For therby wend he to ben gracious.
He cometh to the carpenteres hous,
And still he stant under the shot window ;
Unto his brest it raught, it was so low ;
And soft he cougheth with a semisoun.

What do ye honycombe, swete Alisoun ?
My faire bird, my swete sinamome,
Awaketh, lemman min, and speketh to me.
Ful litel thinken ye upon my wo,
That for your love I swete ther as I go.
No wonder is though that I swelte and swete.
I mourne as doth a lamb after the tete.
Ywis, lemman, I have swiche love-longing,
That like a turtel trewe is my mourning.
I may not ete no more than a maid.

Go fro the window, jacke fool, she said :
As helpe me God, it wol not be, compame.

I love another, or elles I were to blame,
Wel bet than thee by Jesu, Absolon.
Go forth thy way, or I wol cast a ston;
And let me slepe; a twenty divel way.

Alas! (quod Absolon) and wala wa!
That trewe love was ever so yvel besette:
Than kisse me, sin that it may be no bette,
For Jesus love, and for the love of me.

Wilt thou than go thy way therwith? quod she.
Ya certes, lemman, quod this Absolon.
Than make thee redy, (quod she) I come anon.

This Absolon doun set him on his knees,
And saide; I am a lord at all degrees:
For after this I hope ther cometh more;
Lemman, thy grace, and, swete bird, thyn ore.

The window she undoth, and that in haste.
Have don, (quod she) come of, and spede thee
Lest that our neigheboures thee espie.   [faste,

This Absolon gan wipe his mouth ful drie.
Derke was the night, as pitch or as the cole,
And at the window she put out hire hole,
And Absolon him felle ne bet ne wers,
But with his mouth he kist hire naked ers
Ful savorly, er he was ware of this.

Abak he sterte, and thought it was amis,
For wel he wist a woman hath no berd.
He felt a thing all rowe, and long yherd,
And saide; fy, alas! what have I do?

Te he, quod she, and clapt the window to;
And Absolon goth forth a sory pas.

A berd, a berd, said hendy Nicholas;
By goddes *corpus*, this goth faire and wel.

This sely Absolon herd every del,
And on his lippe he gan for anger bite;

And to himself he said, I shal thee quite.

Who rubbeth now, who froteth now his lippes

With dust, with sond, with straw, with cloth, with

But Absolon ? that saith full oft, alas ! [chippes,

My soule betake I unto Sathanas,

But me were lever than all this toun (quod he)

Of this despit awroken for to be.

Alas ! alas ! that I ne had yblent.

His hote love is cold, and all yqueint.

For fro that time that he had kist hire ers,

Of paramours ne raught he not a kers,

For he was heled of his maladie ;

Ful often paramours he gan defie,

And wepe as doth a child that is ybete.

A softe pas he went him over the strete

Until a smith, men callen dan Gerveis,

That in his forge smithed plow-harneis ;

He sharpeth share and cultre besily.

This Absolon knocketh all esily,

And said ; Undo, Gerveis, and that anon.

    What, who art thou ? It am I Absolon.

What ? Absolon, what ? Cristes swete tre,

Why rise ye so rath ? ey *benedicite*,

What eileth you ? some gay girle, God it wote,

Hath brought you thus upon the viretote :

By Seint Neote, ye wote wel what I mene.

    This Absolon ne raughte not a bene

Of all his play ; no word again he yaf.

He hadde more tawe on his distaf

Than Gerveis knew, and saide ; Frend so dere,

That hote culter in the cheminee here

As lene it me, I have therwith to don :

I wol it bring again to thee ful sone.

    Gerveis answered ; Certes, were it gold,

Or in a poke nobles all untold,
Thou shuldest it have, as I am trewe smith.
Ey, Cristes foot, what wol ye don therwith?
Therof, quod Absolon, be as be may;
I shal wel tellen thee another day:
And caught the culter by the colde stele.
Ful soft out at the dore he gan to stele,
And went unto the carpenteres wall.
He coughed first, and knocked therwithall.
Upon the window, right as he did er.

   This Alison answered; Who is ther
That knocketh so? I warrant him a thefe.

   Nay, nay, (quod he) God wot, my swete lefe,
I am thin Absolon, thy dereling.
Of gold (quod he) I have thee brought a ring,
My mother yave it me, so God me save,
Ful fine it is, and therto wel ygrave:
This wol I yeven thee, if thou me kisse.

   This Nicholas was risen for to pisse,
And thought he wolde amenden all the jape,
He shulde kisse his ers er that he scape:
And up the window did he hastily,
And out his ers he putteth prively
Over the buttok, to the hanche bon.
And therwith spake this clerk, this Absolon,
Speke swete bird, I n'ot not wher thou art.

   This Nicholas anon let fleen a fart,
As gret as it had ben a thonder dint,
That with the stroke he was wel nie yblint:
And he was redy with his yren hote,
And Nicholas amid the ers he smote.

   Off goth the skinne an hondbrede al aboute.
The hote culter brenned so his toute,
That for the smert he wened for to die;

I   I

As he were wood, for wo he gan to crie,
Help, water, water, help for Goddes herte.

This carpenter out of his slomber sterte,
And herd on crie water, as he were wood,
And thought, alas, now cometh Noes flood.
He set him up withouten wordes mo,
And with his axe he smote the cord atwo;
And doun goth all; he fond neyther to selle
Ne breed ne ale, til he came to the selle,
Upon the flore, and ther aswoune he lay.

Up sterten Alison and Nicholay,
And crieden, out and harow! in the strete.

The neigheboures bothe smale and grete
In rannen, for to gauren on this man,
That yet aswoune lay, bothe pale and wan:
For with the fall he brosten hath his arm.
But stonden he must unto his owen harm,
For whan he spake, he was anon bore doun
With hendy Nicholas and Alisoun.
They tolden every man that he was wood;
He was agaste so of Noes flood
Thurgh fantasie, that of his vanitee
He had ybought him kneding tubbes three,
And had hem honged in the roof above;
And that he praied hem for Goddes love
To sitten in the roof *par compagnie.*

The folk gan laughen at his fantasie.
Into the roof they kyken, and they gape,
And turned all his harm into a jape.
For what so that this carpenter answerd,
It was for nought, no man his reson herd.
With othes gret he was so sworne adoun,
That he was holden wood in all the toun.
For everich clerk anon right held with other;

They said, the man was wood, my leve brother;
And every wight gan laughen at this strif.

Thus swived was the carpenteres wif,
For all his keping, and his jalousie;
And Absolon hath kist hire nether eye;
And Nicholas is scalded in the toute.
This tale is don, and God save all the route.

The Reves Prologue.

WHAN folk han laughed at this nice cas
Of Absolon and hendy Nicholas,
Diverse folk diversely they saide,
But for the more part they lought and plaide;
Ne at this tale I saw no man him greve,
But it were only Osewold the Reve.
Because he was of carpenteres craft,
A litel ire is in his herte ylaft;
He gan to grutch and blamen it a lite.
So the ik, quod he, ful wel coude I him quite
With blering of a proude milleres eye,
If that me list to speke of ribaudrie.
But ik am olde; me list not play for age;
Gras time is don, my foddre is now forage.
This white top writeth min olde yeres;
Min herte is also mouled as min heres;
But if I fare as doth an open-ers;
That ilke fruit is ever lenger the wers,
Til it be roten in mullok, or in stre.

We olde men, I drede, so faren we,
Til we be roten, can we not be ripe;

We hoppe alway, while that the world wol pipe;
For in our will ther stiketh ever a nayl,
To have an hore hed and a grene tayl,
As hath a leke; for though our might be gon,
Our will desireth folly ever in on:
For whan we may not don, than wol we speken,
Yet in our ashen cold is fire yreken.

Foure gledes han we, which I shal devise,
Avaunting, lying, anger, and covetise.
These foure sparkes longen unto elde.
Our olde limes mow wel ben unwelde,
But will ne shal not faillen, that is sothe.
And yet have I alway a coltes tothe,
As many a yere as it is passed henne,
Sin that my tappe of lif began to renne.
For sikerly, whan I was borne, anon
Deth drow the tappe of lif, and let it gon:
And ever sith hath so the tappe yronne,
Til that almost all empty is the tonne.
The streme of lif now droppeth on the chimbe.
The sely tonge may wel ringe and chimbe
Of wretchednesse, that passed is ful yore:
With olde folk, save dotage, is no more.

Whan that our Hoste had herd this sermoning,
He gan to speke as lordly as a king,
And sayde; What amounteth all this wit?
What? shall we speke all day of holy writ?
The divel made a Reve for to preche,
Or of a souter a shipman, or a leche.

Say forth thy tale, and tary not the time:
Lo Depeford, and it is half way prime:
Lo Grenewich, ther many a shrew is inne.
It were al time thy tale to beginne.

Now, sires, quod this Osewold the Reve,

I pray you alle, that ye not you greve,
Though I answere, and somdel set his howve,
For leful is with force, force off to showve.

This dronken Miller hath ytold us here,
How that begiled was a carpentere,
Paraventure in scorne, for I am on:
And by your leve, I shal him quite anon.
Right in his cherles termes wol I speke.
I pray to God his necke mote to-breke.
He can wel in min eye seen a stalk,
But in his owen he cannot seen a balk.

The Reves Tale.

AT Trompington, not fer fro Cantebrigge,
Ther goth a brook, and over that a brigge,
Upon the whiche brook ther stont a melle:
And this is veray sothe, that I you telle.
A miller was ther dwelling many a day,
As any peacok he was proude and gay:
Pipen he coude, and fishe, and nettes bete,
And turnen cuppes, and wrastlen wel, and shete.
Ay by his belt he bare a long pavade,
And of a swerd ful trenchant was the blade.
A joly popper bare he in his pouche;
Ther n'as no man for peril dorst him touche.
A Shefeld thwitel bare he in his hose.
Round was his face, and camuse was his nose.
As pilled as an ape was his skull.
He was a market-beter at the full.
Ther dorste no wight hond upon him legge,

That he ne swore he shuld anon abegge.

A thefe he was forsoth, of corn and mele,
And that a slie, and usant for to stele.
His name was hoten deinous Simekin.
A wif he hadde, comen of noble kin:
The person of the toun hire father was.
With hire he yaf ful many a panne of bras,
For that Simkin shuld in his blood allie.
She was yfostered in a nonnerie:
For Simkin wolde no wif, as he sayde,
But she were wel ynourished, and a mayde,
To saven his estat of yemanrie:
And she was proud, and pert as is a pie.
A ful faire sight was it upon hem two.
On holy dayes beforne hire wold he go
With his tipet ybounde about his hed;
And she came after in a gite of red,
And Simkin hadde hosen of the same.
Ther dorste no wight clepen hire but Dame:
Was non so hardy, that went by the way,
That with hire dorste rage or ones play,
But if he wold be slain of Simekin
With pavade, or with knif, or bodekin.
(For jalous folk ben perilous evermo:
Algate they wold hir wives wenden so.)
And eke for she was somdel smoterlich,
She was as digne as water in a dich,
And al so ful of hoker, and of bismare.
Hire thoughte that a ladie shuld hire spare,
What for hire kinrede, and hire nortelrie
That she had lerned in the nonnerie.

A doughter hadden they betwix hem two
Of twenty yere, withouten any mo,
Saving a child that was of half yere age,

In cradle it lay, and was a propre page.
This wenche thicke and wel ygrowen was,
With camuse nose, and eyen grey as glas;
With buttokes brode, and brestes round and hie;
But right faire was hire here, I wol nat lie.

The person of the toun, for she was faire,
In purpos was to maken hire his haire
Both of his catel, and of his mesuage,
And strange he made it of hire mariage.
His purpos was for to bestowe hire hie
Into som worthy blood of ancestrie.
For holy chirches good mote ben despended
On holy chirches blood that is descended.
Therfore he wolde his holy-blood honoure,
Though that he holy chirche shuld devoure.

Gret soken hath this miller out of doute
With whete and malt, of all the land aboute;
And namely ther was a gret college
Men clepe the Soler hall at Cantebrege,
Ther was hir whete and eke hir malt yground.
And on a day it happed in a stound,
Sike lay the manciple on a maladie,
Men wenden wisly that he shulde die.
For which this miller stale both mele and corn
An hundred times more than beforn.
For therbeforn he stale but curteisly,
But now he was a thefe outrageously.
For which the wardein chidde and made fare,
But therof set the miller not a tare;
He craked bost, and swore it n'as not so.

Than were ther yonge poure scoleres two,
That dwelten in the halle of which I say;
Testif they were, and lusty for to play;
And only for hir mirth and revelrie

Upon the wardein besily they crie,
To yeve hem leve but a litel stound,
To gon to mille, and seen hir corn yground:
And hardily they dorsten lay hir necke,
The miller shuld not stele hem half a pecke
Of corn by sleighte, ne by force hem reve.

And at the last the wardein yave hem leve:
John highte that on, and Alein highte that other,
Of o toun were they born, that highte Strother,
Fer in the North, I can not tellen where.

This Alein maketh redy all his gere,
And on a hors the sak he cast anon:
Forth goth Alein the clerk, and also John,
With good swerd and with bokeler by hir side.
John knew the way, him neded not no guide,
And at the mille the sak adoun he laith.

Alein spake first; All haile, Simond, in faith,
How fares thy faire doughter, and thy wif?

Alein, welcome (quod Simkin) by my lif,
And John also: how now, what do ye here?
By God, Simond, (quod John) nede has no pere.
Him behoves serve himself that has na swain,
Or elles he is a fool, as clerkes sain.
Our manciple I hope he wol be ded,
Swa werkes ay the wanges in his hed:
And therfore is I come, and eke Alein,
To grind our corn and cary it hame agein:
I pray you spede us henen that ye may.

It shal be don (quod Simkin) by my fay.
What wol ye don while that it is in hand?
By God, right by the hopper wol I stand,
(Quod John) and seen how that the corn gas in.
Yet saw I never by my fader kin,
How that the hopper wagges til and fra.

Alein answered; John, and wolt thou swa?
Than wol I be benethe by my croun,
And see how that the mele falles adoun
In til the trogh, that shal be my disport:
For, John, in faith I may ben of your sort;
I is as ill a miller as is ye.

This miller smiled at hir nicetee,
And thought, all this n'is don but for a wile.
They wenen that no man may hem begile,
But by my thrift yet shal I blere hir eie,
For all the sleighte in hir philosophie.
The more queinte knakkes that they make,
The more wol I stele whan that I take.
In stede of flour yet wol I yeve hem bren.
The gretest clerkes ben not the wisest men,
As whilom to the wolf thus spake the mare:
Of all hir art ne count I not a tare.

Out at the dore he goth ful prively,
Whan that he saw his time, softely.
He loketh up and doun, til he hath found
The clerkes hors, ther as he stood ybound
Behind the mille, under a levesell:
And to the hors he goth him faire and well,
And stripeth of the bridel right anon.

And whan the hors was laus, he gan to gon
Toward the fen, ther wilde mares renne,
And forth, with wehee, thurgh thick and thinne.
This miller goth again, no word he said,
But doth his note, and with these clerkes plaid,
Till that hir corn was faire and wel yground.
And whan the mele is sacked and ybound,
This John goth out, and fint his hors away,
And gan to crie, harow and wala wa!
Our hors is lost: Alein, for Goddes banes,

Step on thy feet; come of, man, al at anes:
Alas! our wardein has his palfrey lorn.

This Alein al forgat both mele and corn;
Al was out of his mind his husbandrie:
What, whilke way is he gon? he gan to crie.

The wif came leping inward at a renne,
She sayd; Alas! youre hors goth to the fenne
With wilde mares, as fast as he may go.
Unthank come on his hand that bond him so,
And he that better shuld have knit the rein.

Alas! (quod John) Alein, for Christes pein
Lay doun thy swerd, and I shal min alswa.
I is ful wight, God wate, as is a ra.
By Goddes saule he shal not scape us bathe.
Why ne had thou put the capel in the lathe?
Ill haile, Alein, by God thou is a fonne.

These sely clerkes han ful fast yronne
Toward the fen, bothe Alein and eke John:
And whan the miller saw that they were gon,
He half a bushel of hir flour hath take,
And bad his wif go knede it in a cake.
He sayd; I trow, the clerkes were aferde.
Yet can a miller make a clerkes berde,
For all his art. Ye, let hem gon hir way.
Lo wher they gon. Ye, let the children play:
They get him not so lightly by my croun.

These sely clerkes rennen up and doun
With kepe, kepe; stand, stand; jossa, warderere.
Ga whistle thou, and I shal kepe him here.
But shortly, til that it was veray night
They coude not, though they did all hir might,
Hir capel catch, he ran alway so fast:
Til in a diche they caught him at the last.

Wery and wet, as bestes in the rain,

Cometh sely John, and with him cometh Alein.
Alas (quod John) the day that I was borne!
Now are we driven til hething and til scorne.
Our corn is stolne, men wol us fonnes calle,
Both the wardein, and eke our felawes alle,
And namely the miller, wala wa!

   Thus plaineth John, as he goth by the way
Toward the mille, and bayard in his hond.
The miller sitting by the fire he fond,
For it was night, and forther might they nought,
But for the love of God they him besought
Of herberwe and of ese, as for hir peny.

   The miller saide agen, if ther be any,
Swiche as it is, yet shull ye have your part.
Myn hous is streit, but ye have lerned art;
Ye can by argumentes maken a place
A mile brode, of twenty foot of space.
Let see now if this place may suffice,
Or make it roume with speche, as is your gise.
Now, Simond, (said this John) by Seint Cuth-
Ay is thou mery, and that is faire answerd. [berd
I have herd say, man sal take of twa thinges,
Slike as he findes, or slike as he bringes.
But specially I pray thee, hoste dere,
Gar us have mete and drinke, and make us chere,
And we sal paien trewely at the full:
With empty hand, men may na haukes tull.
Lo here our silver redy for to spend.

   This miller to the toun his doughter send
For ale and bred, and rosted hem a goos,
And bond hir hors, he shuld no more go loos:
And in his owen chambre hem made a bedde,
With shetes and with chalons faire yspredde,
Nat from his owen bed ten foot or twelve:

Unhardy is unsely, thus men say.
    And up he rose, and softely he went
Unto the cradel, and in his hand it hent,
And bare it soft unto his beddes fete.
Sone after this the wif hire routing lete,
And gan awake, and went hire out to pisse,
And came again, and gan the cradel misse,
And groped here and ther, but she fond non.
Alas! (quod she) I had almost misgon.
I had almost gon to the clerkes bedde.
Ey *benedicite*, than had I foule yspedde.
And forth she goth, til she the cradel fond.
She gropeth alway forther with hire hond,
And fond the bed, and thoughte nat but good,
Because that the cradel by it stood,
And n'iste wher she was, for it was derk,
But faire and wel she crept in by the clerk,
And lith ful still, and wold han caught a slepe.
Within a while this John the clerk up lepe,
And on this goode wif he laieth on sore ;
So mery a fit ne had she nat ful yore.
He priketh hard and depe, as he were mad.
    This joly lif han these two clerkes lad,
Til that the thridde cok began to sing.
Alein wex werie in the morwening,
For he had swonken all the longe night,
And sayd ; Farewel, Malkin, my swete wight.
The day is come, I may no longer bide,
But evermo, wher so I go or ride,
I is thin awen clerk, so have I hele.
Now, dere lemman, quod she, go farewele :
But or thou go, o thing I wol thee tell.
Whan that thou wendest homeward by the mell,
Right at the entree of the dore behind